LIKE A MIGHTY RIVER

also by the author

The Jesus Factor

The Light and the Glory, with Peter Marshall

The Land of Milk and Honey, with Bill Basansky

Babunia, with Bill Basansky

Walking and Leaping, with Merlin Carothers

LIKE A MIGHTY RIVER

David Manuel

ROCK HARBOR PRESS
ORLEANS, MASSACHUSETTS

289.93

Copyright © 1977 by David Manuel
Library of Congress Catalog Card Number 77-90948
All Rights Reserved
Published by Rock Harbor Press
Printed in the United States of America

Aknowledgements

I need to apologize to all the groups and workshops which I did not have the opportunity to cover, and the old friends whom I did not have a chance to interview. The omission was not intentional. There are a number of advantages to using the first-person point of view, but one disadvantage is that one person can be in only one place at a time. That I was not always in the right place at the right time became apparent to me, and for this I ask your forgiveness. As it was, we came away with far more material than we could possibly use — enough for a book four times this size — and were subsequently sent even more. On that score, I must also ask the forgiveness of all who did contribute interviews and anecdotes to the book, but whose contributions, because of the limitations of space, do not appear in these pages.

I would also like to acknowledge my gratitude to the planning committee, for their confidence and support; to the CRS staff, for going out of their way to help us in every way that they could; to John Sorensen, our photographer, who did yeoman's work on the field and in the darkroom; to Carol Showalter, for being an extra pair of eyes and ears, and speaking truth when I needed to hear it; to Pete Borel, Harry Lunn, and our other Kansas City helpers; and to my partner Dean Smith, who has been a true brother in Christ, and is becoming a first-class reporter.

Above all, I need to acknowledge my utter dependence upon the grace and mercy — and patience — of God, whom I am finally learning to trust.

October 1977   David Manuel
                                 Cape Cod, Massachusetts

"In honor preferring one another..."

To those who served,

    this book is dedicated.

1

Kansas City

I can't remember now, exactly why I called Pete Borel. I think it was in connection with CBA — the annual convention of the Christian Booksellers Association that was coming up in the middle of the next month, July 10, to be exact. This year, it was to be in Kansas City, and my friend and publishing partner, Dean Smith, and I were going out for it, to launch our first Rock Harbor book.

"You know," Pete said, "you really ought to stay in town for the Charismatic Conference. It begins five days later, and it's probably going to be the most important thing of its kind in modern history."

I was used to such exaggeration in advance of Christian conferences, but this one in Kansas City — this one had a different feel to it . . . "They're projecting for sixty thousand people," Pete was saying, "which means it will be the biggest —"

"But they'll be mostly Catholics, won't they?" I interrupted him. "I mean, aren't the Catholics running it?"

"Well, yes, they're providing the organization. But it's not like that, really. Don Schmit and I have been sitting in on the planning committee's meetings, and they're truly ecumenical. Brick Bradford's here, and Larry Christenson, and Carlton Spencer, and Bob Mumford, and Vinson Synan, and Bob Hawn —"

"Okay, okay," I laughed, "so it *is* ecumenical. But do they really mean to have each denomination's own Charismatic convention going on simultaneously?"

Now it was Pete's turn to laugh. "That's about the size of it. At the 1977 Conference on the Charismatic Renewal in the Christian Churches, the different denominations — the Presbyterians, the Episcopalians, the Messianic Jews, et cetera — will have their own conferences in the mornings. The afternoons will be given over to workshops, and then everyone will get together at Arrowhead Stadium in the evening."

"Well," I said, "it's certainly going to be the biggest something — but, Pete, if it's all that unusual, is anyone doing a book on the conference?" I hadn't meant it seriously, but the silence on the other end indicated he was taking it that way.

"No, I don't believe there is," he paused. "But it's an awfully good idea. In fact, I'm surprised they haven't thought of it. Tell you what: why don't I ask them?"

"You mean, they're meeting now?" Suddenly things seemed to be accelerating into a new dimension.

"Yes, by coincidence, you happened to get me during one of their few breaks, speaking of which, I've got to get back in there. They're only in town for two days, and this is the last planning session they'll be able to have until just before the conference, so they've got a tight agenda."

"Okay," I said, "just for fun, let me get some specs together, and I'll call you back."

"Better make it late tonight, or you won't get me at all," and with that we said goodbye.

I stared at the phone, sitting silent on my desk now, like a smug red toad. What were we getting into? Of all the conference books I knew of, and some of them were really beautiful, I did not know of one which had wound up in the black. Maybe those bigger, older publishing houses could afford it, but even a mild setback at this stage of Rock Harbor's precarious birth could spell the end, almost before the beginning.

Lord, are you in this, I prayed; is this your will for us at this time? But even as I formed the words, I knew that I was not going to get the red-light/green-light guidance that I would so like to have had. No, like certain other major decisions, this was going to have to be decided on faith.

Well, the first thing to do was call Dean. Dean and I were both members of the Community of Jesus, an ecumenical Charismatic community on Cape Cod. For about four years, Dean and his wife Virginia, and my wife Barbara and I, had felt that God was leading us to enter a partnership to publish Christian books. Now it was beginning to happen.

"You've got to be out of your tree!" I could imagine Dean saying, "we're already in hock up to our eyeballs to publish our first book, and now you want to —" But as was so often the case, how I imagined a thing was not at all the way it went.

"Sounds interesting," Dean said. "Why don't you call the printer and find out what it would cost to do, and how many we'd have to sell to break even?"

Somewhat taken aback, I proceeded to do just that. But before I could call, I needed to have something to tell the printer. Lord, I prayed, at least give me some idea of what ballpark we're playing in. What came to mind was a hardcover book of just under two hundred pages, with at least sixteen pages of photographs, that would sell for less than five dollars. And we were to turn over to the conference a generous percentage off the top, to help defray their mountainous expenses.

Then came the sixty-four-dollar question: how many copies could we count on selling? The figure that came to mind was 6000.

I called our printer and found that on our actual cost-out-of-pocket, we would break even at 4500 copies. How many did we need to sell, in order to cover the time we would spend covering the conference and then writing, editing and publishing the book? In the area of 6000 copies. That 'coincidence' should have been a clear indication that God was in charge, and I should have been elated. But instead, I was almost in a state of dread. I felt like I had just gotten into the front seat of a roller coaster. Any moment now, the attendant would lock the bar across my lap, and the car would begin to move . . .

I called Pete that night with the specifications. He said he would try to mention the proposal the next day, but it looked doubtful. They still had an enormous amount to cover, and Kevin Ranaghan, who was chairing the committee, was doing his best to see that they finished their agenda by four, when they were all due to fly home. It could well be that there simply wouldn't be time, in which case it would be almost impossible to get a consensus before the conference actually began. I tried to sound concerned, but inside I was relieved. Now, if anything came of it, it would have to be God, and since that was so unlikely, I had no trouble falling asleep.

The next day, I must have asked the Lord a dozen times if He was *sure* we would sell 6000 copies at the conference, and each time the answer seemed to come back: between five and six. The last time I asked, I was in the chapel, taking my hour on our twenty-four-hour prayer vigil, and I glanced up at the clock. It was five minutes to six. I shut up after that — for about an hour.

Late that night, the phone rang. It was Pete: they'd approved the idea and asked for a full presentation in writing. "It was really amazing!" the voice on the other end of the phone exclaimed. "They finished the agenda at five minutes to four. Kevin asked if there were any last questions or points to be brought up. I raised my hand, he recognized me, and I told him of the proposal. And everyone liked it, though many of them didn't know who you were, and no one had ever heard of Rock Harbor Press. It was the Lord, all right!"

"Yeah, I guess it was," I said weakly, wishing I could be more enthusiastic. The roller coaster attendant was checking now, to make sure all lap bars and doors were secured.

The next few days were a blur of preparations, as we got ready for CBA and also got our presentation together. On one point we were emphatic: the only way to capture the full drama of the conference was to tell the story from the personal point of view of a participant. This would mean that it would be necessarily selective, as there was no way one person could cover ten denominational conferences, let alone all the workshops. We would concentrate on those experiences which would be common to everyone, such as the evenings at Arrowhead Stadium, and trust the Holy Spirit to put us where we were supposed to be, the rest of the time.

We were just loading our station wagon with cases of books, when I was called in the house for a phone call. It was Kevin Ranaghan. I had never met him, but his voice was smooth and extremely well-modulated. He sounded like a super-professional — someone very much in control, who never lost his cool. I was impressed and perhaps the slightest bit intimidated. What he was saying was that the committee liked our presentation, and as of that moment, we had a green light. He did want to meet with us, though, and by coincidence, we would be driving right by South Bend, Indiana, on our way to Chicago and then Kansas City. Could we get together for lunch on Friday?

"We've taken over the old La Salle Hotel," he said.

"Some of the People of Praise community live on the top floor, and we have our offices in the rest. Shall we say around 11:30? Wonderful, we'll look forward to seeing you then."

And that was it. With a slight jolt, the roller coaster started its ascent. I could almost hear the clacking of the chain, as we were drawn smoothly, relentlessly upward.

"Turn off here," Dean said, as we approached the next exit on I-80. He had grown up in central Illinois, and was able to point out portions of the Notre Dame campus. I was surprised at the thrill that went through me. It must have been thirty years since I had learned the Notre Dame fight song in summer camp and pretended I was Johnny Lujack, fading back, arm cocked, peering down field for a receiver to break into the open. And then there were those great old movies that glorified virtues which seemed to have gone sadly out of fashion in today's world . . .

I grinned; even the buildings, in dignified gray Gothic, encrusted with ivy, looked the part. It was like we were driving through a movie set. I imagined a Knute Rockne team running out on the field in green jerseys and leather helmets, a tremendous roar filling the stadium, as 60,000 spectators rose to their feet. It was said that on Saturday afternoon, Notre Dame was the alma mater of every Catholic in America who had a radio. It was also the secret first choice of practically every young Protestant boy who ever thought he might one day go to college . . .

"There she is," Dean observed, as the La Salle Hotel hove into view. I glanced at my watch — 11:10 — it was nice to be a whole twenty minutes early, for a change. We parked and walked over to the eight-story, sandstone building, where we were directed to the third floor. There, we were put at ease by a gracious receptionist and told that Kevin would be with us in a few minutes.

From where I sat, I could partially see into what appeared to be an accounting office, where a great deal of activity was taking place. In fact, judging from the number of people passing up and down the corridor, and the number of calls lighting up the receptionist's switchboard, this had to be the busiest office I had been in in some time. And yet there was, at the same time, an unusual feeling of peace about the premises; no one could have guessed that the conference was less than two weeks away.

In came a tall, smiling man with graying hair and steel-rimmed glasses. This was Kevin Ranaghan, and he led us back to his office, a converted corner room, which must have been one of the more attractive accommodations of the old hotel. The La Salle, in the midst of renovation, had gone bankrupt, and had, through one of those complicated, beautiful moves of the Spirit, passed into the hands of the Charismatic Renewal Services, for a fraction of its real, but unrealizable, worth.

What — and who — were the Charismatic Renewal Services? The Charismatic Renewal had come to the Catholic Church comparatively late, in 1967, when some Catholic students at Duquesne University in Pittsburgh went on a retreat and prayed for — and received — the Baptism in the Holy Spirit. That was the beginning, and I could remember reading of one of their earliest conferences at Notre Dame, in 1969, which drew some five hundred brave souls. Since then, the growth of the Renewal in the Catholic Church had been dramatic; last year, more than 30,000 ignored the rain to attend the conference in the football stadium.

They had come a long ways in a very short time, and those responsible for organizing the conferences had learned an enormous amount about the logistics of putting on a major conference. Out of this experience had evolved the Charismatic Renewal Services, a non-profit corporation, staffed for the most part by members of two ecumenical (albeit largely Roman Catholic) communities, the People of Praise in South Bend, and the Word of God in Ann Arbor, Michigan. Most of the administrative end of things was handled in South Bend, while Ann Arbor provided the media input — tapes, records, books, programs, and the magazine, *New Covenant*.

In a sense, the People of Praise community had a corporate call on it, to serve the Body of Christ through the CRS. There were more than eight hundred members, living in approximately forty households throughout the city. The numbers were a little breathtaking to me, and I realized that I had gotten a bit insular in my thinking. Our own community, in which I'd lived for six years, numbered only a hundred and fifty in fifteen households. I knew of the Word of God, which had some twelve hundred members, and I'd been to Houston, to cover the Redeemer community for *Logos*, which three years ago had had some 440 members in forty-three households. But I had no idea that there were at least a dozen more, as large or larger than ours, and heaven only knew how many smaller ones.

Kevin got up from behind his desk and said, "Come on, I'll show you around the place," and we quickly got up and followed him. The tour became a whirl of computers and accounting rooms, of registration packets going out, and figures being tallied and graphed. Everyone seemed to be working at maximum capacity, and yet everyone also seemed to be genuinely happy and quick with a smile. It didn't take a lot of discernment to see why; they were "on the stretch for God," as George Whitefield had once put it. They were doing what they were called to do and were being graced to do more than they were capable of doing, and they knew it.

In one room, where a computer was chunking out names and addresses, Kevin picked up the latest registration figures. "As of last Friday, we have processed thirty-one thousand registrations. That means we are going to fall short of our original projection of sixty thousand, but just how many we're going to wind up with, no one knows for sure." He pointed to a large chart on the wall. "If past registration patterns can be relied on, we should level off at around forty thousand." He chuckled. "But so far, this conference has broken all the rules. Its performance is so unlike anything we've ever experienced before, it's impossible to predict, especially since the rate of registrations now seems to be accelerating. Anyway, after today, we're not processing any more through the mail. We're telling them to wait until Kansas City, and we'll process them at Arrowhead Stadium, Wednesday."

Back in his office, he showed us how the registrations broke down by denominations. As I had anticipated, there was a preponderance of Catholics, some thirteen thousand, five hundred. But there was also a substantial number of Lutherans, around two thousand; Episcopalians, fifteen hundred; Presbyterians, over a thousand; and Baptists, Mennonites, Pentecostals, Methodists, and Messianic Jews, with the largest block after the Catholics being the Nondenominationals, at six thousand. "Actually," Kevin said, "we think there may well be quite a number of people who have registered as Nondenominationals, because they want to be free to float around — not that they couldn't, anyway." He got up. "Shall we have some lunch?"

The coffee shop, which had come with the hotel, was bright and cheery, and also staffed by the People of Praise. We took a table away from the main traffic flow, and as soon as I had my tape recorder set up, Dean said, "Tell us about the conference in your own words. How did it come about?"

Kevin thought for a moment, before answering. "It's the

culmination of something that has been coming for a long time. Back in 1974, at the Notre Dame conference, Ralph Martin gave what we've come to call the 'Three Streams' talk, in which he delineated the three main streams of the Charismatic Renewal — the Classical Pentecostals, the Neo-Pentecostals, and the Catholic Pentecostals. And then he shared the vision of bringing these three streams together, to form one mighty river of the Spirit.

"In a sense, that talk was the inspiration for the Kansas City conference. Because after it, a number of us who were there felt that it was God's desire — and time — to bring these streams together. This was a particularly welcome word for the People of Praise community, for we had always felt that the Lord had raised us up as a community, to work responsibly towards Christian unity. CRS was a fruit of that work, and at CRS, we had the capacity to respond to such a word and do something to promote the bringing of these streams together in a conference."

The waitress had come for our order, but she waited politely until Kevin finished his point. "Which is *not* to say that the idea originated with us. It had been kicking around for several years, and about the same time as Ralph's talk, Vinson Synan's *Charismatic Bridges* was published, calling for essentially the same thing." And now the waitress took our order — three chef's salads and three Tabs.

"But it needed one body to be committed to actually doing it," Kevin resumed, "and after Ralph's talk, we felt we had the timing of the Lord. It seemed right to start sharing the vision with a number of other Charismatic leaders, and gradually this was how the Kansas City conference came to pass."

How did the planning committee actually come into being? "Well, I initially contacted the men who were in the kind of position I was in, on their respective denominational committees — Larry Christenson, Bob Hawn, Brick Bradford, Nelson Litwiller, and so on. Then the Charismatic fellowships in the various denominations decided that, rather than have their own annual meetings, they would throw in their lot with us. It was a gamble, because a lot of them depended on their annual conferences to meet their financial needs, and now they would have to trust the CRS to set up their conferences for them. What's more, they have agreed that should the conference go," he hesitated, "bankrupt, they will make up the deficit in proportion to their respective registrations, by going back to their people and raising the money."

I was about to ask what sort of deficit, if any, they were presently facing, when Dean speculated about the difficulty of deciding which denomination would meet where, or what workshop would be in which location when. Had chauvinism ever reared its ugly head? "I think what has made the planning committee work was that we decided to be brothers and not committee members. We have been committed to discerning God's will for the conference as a whole, and have not tried for any kind of denominational balance on the program. We want the people to speak whom we feel that God wants to have speak. And you know, the denominational interests seem to have sorted themselves out beautifully."

Could he give an example? "Well, there is a certain set of facilities which might be termed slightly less desirable than certain other sets. We've always known that somebody was going to have to use them. But no one ever had to be asked; the morning that we had to assign them, three people just volunteered, and everything fell into place . . . the whole thing has been like that, a real spirit of dying to self and deferring to the common good. If this conference is a success, one of the major reasons is going to be the coming together of the leadership at this level. And I think that says something about the future — about how it really is possible for us to work together and to submit to one another without fear."

We considered dessert then, and decided against it. Almost everyone we had talked to about the conference, whether they were going themselves or not, regarded this one as something special, different from any conference that had ever happened before — why? What was responsible for the mystique about this one? Kevin gazed out the window. "First of all, it's truly ecumenical. It is *not* a gathering of people who have come out of their churches and are coming as individuals to another Charismatic get-together. The Kansas City conference will actually be ten conferences in one, with each Charismatic denominational association holding its own annual conference in the morning sessions. In the afternoon, there will be open workshops, nearly thirty of them, with teachers from all denominations. And in the evening, all of us will come together at Arrowhead Stadium, to join in common worship and be truly one in the Spirit." He paused to take a drink.

"We are *not* trying to blend all denominations into one," Kevin emphasized, "or ignore the obvious differences, which have been there since the Reformation and Counter-Reformation. But in Kansas City, you will see people choosing to focus on the positives, on the unity which already exists among us to a surprising degree — on Jesus Christ."

The Lord, then, would have this conference be a witness to the whole Body of Christ and the world at large, that such unity is possible? "Yes. We have a tremendous responsibility to be a prophetic body within the Church. I believe that the Lord will speak to us directly at the conference, and not just us Charismatics, but all who call themselves by His name."

How on earth were they ever going to cope with prophetic utterances or tongues and interpretation, in a congregation of upwards of forty thousand? "The Lord worked that out for us in our previous conferences at Notre Dame. We have instituted something that we call the Word Gifts Group."

He paused and smiled. "I can already hear people saying, 'Leave it to the Catholics to invent something like a Word Gifts Group!' But it works! We take forty or fifty men and women who have demonstrated in their local groups or churches that they have considerable spiritual maturity, as well as the gift of prophecy or interpretation. These people will pray together by themselves for an hour before the evening meeting, and then will sit on the speakers' platform. And when they receive a prophecy or a vision or an exhortation from Scripture, they will share it with one of the group's leaders who, in turn, will pass it on for insertion in the program, when and if it seems right. But we will also encourage anyone in the stadium who receives a prophecy or a vision, to write it down and bring it to the information desk. We will pray over them and bring some of them forth, also. We don't want to stifle the Spirit," Kevin concluded, "but this has got to be handled in an orderly way."

"Like a mighty river," Dean, who had been largely silent, suddenly said out of nowhere.

"Huh?" I looked over at him, and he appeared to be as surprised as we were.

"Like a Mighty River — that's going to be the title of our book," he explained. "It came to me while you were talking. It just sort of bubbled up," he added, a trifle self-consciously.

I was speechless. Dean was usually about as practical and down-to-earth as a person could be. He just wasn't the sort to go around bubbling up titles. But then a lot of unusual things had already begun to come out of Dean on this trip, and that would be just the way the Lord would give the title, through a least likely source. And it fit, when you stopped to think about it —

"Look at the Mississippi," Dean said, warming to his subject. "Up in Minnesota, it's so narrow, you can jump across it. But as it goes down through the heart of the country and is fed by the Illinois and the Missouri and the Ohio, and all those other tributaries . . ." We all fell silent. I couldn't believe it; we had our title. And it was God, all right; getting the right title was often the hardest single thing about doing a book. Sometimes a book would be all the way to the printer's before it got its title, and some books never did get the right title. But we had ours now, well ahead of time — although not a moment too soon, because we would have to start promoting it right away.

"Incidentally," Kevin said, as we got up from the table, to return to his office, "you ought to get ahold of a copy of Ralph Martin's *Fire on the Earth*, a short book which is an extension of his 'Three Streams' talk." And so I picked one up, in the bookstore across the hall.

Back in his office, we were joined by John Boughton, who would be in charge of the three conference bookstores, and who wanted to go over the order form, which Rock Harbor Press was to provide. The conference would do the promoting, and would collect order forms and payment at the bookstores; we were to take care of everything else.

"Well," said Kevin, "I think that takes care of everything, unless you can think of something we haven't covered. We're satisfied, if you are." We nodded, and that was the sum total of our arrangement — no contract, not even a letter of agreement.

It was time to go, but there was one thing we hadn't covered, and I knew that if I didn't mention it, for the next two weeks I would suffer the tortures of the cowardly. "Kevin, we need to sell six thousand copies, to break even on our time and everything . . ."

"Well, you shouldn't have any trouble selling that quantity."

"I know," I said, ashamed of the shallowness of my faith, "but supposing we don't. We're looking at a possible loss of several thousand dollars," I persisted.

Kevin looked right at me for a moment, before answering. "Have you any idea of the deficit *we're* looking at right now? Even with thirty-five thousand registrations, we're going to be short by $252,000!"

My eyes widened, and I made no reply. "But this is God's conference," he reassured me. "He's going to take care of it. And He'll take care of your book, too." And he got up and came around from behind his desk to say goodbye.

The last thing he said, as we were going out the door was, "I read somewhere that the first white men to discover the Mississippi were missionaries. You know what they named it? 'The River of the Holy Spirit.'"

We were elated at that. But my joy sighed away like the air out of a leaking tire, and by the time we were outside, I'd gone flat. Sitting in the car while Dean drove out of town, it seemed to me that the roller coaster was click-click-clicking, and we were rapidly approaching the summit.

2

Over the Top

Through the windshield of the wagon, the heat of the bright July afternoon seemed to shimmer up from the pavement of I-55, as we drove south for St. Louis, on our way to Kansas City. We rode along in silence mostly, with Dean occasionally reminiscing, for this was the land in which he had grown up. To me, it appeared to be unbearably flat; I had always heard that it was, of course, but it's one thing to fly over it and quite another to drive through it hour after hour.

But Dean loved it. "Corn should be higher than that by now," he observed, as we drove past one of the endless fields. "The drought must be getting to them." I tried to imagine the height of an elephant's eye — but how big an elephant did you use? Yet even I could tell that the corn we had passed in Indiana, the day before, had been taller and greener. My mind drifted off to an episode that had happened a number of years before, in the ministry of my friend Peter Marshall. He had been invited to hold a three-day mission in West Texas, in a county that hadn't had any rain at all in months. They had prayed and prayed, but the heavens had remained as closed as a brass drum, and the ground beneath them had cracked open, the crops withering and turning brown under the relentless sun.

"You don't need prayer," Peter had told them. "You need repentance. On the plane coming in, the Lord seemed to be saying to me that until there's some real heart-searching and forgiveness and repentance, there isn't going to be any rain." For the next three days, he preached a strong, convicting message on repentance, and counseled individuals privately, and it turned out that there was indeed much that had been stuffed down and buried and otherwise put out of mind. But there was also the beginnings of repentance, and while Peter was still there, a rain shower came. It didn't last long, and it was a long time before it rained again, but it was a beginning...

Funny to think of that, after all these years . . . Practically the whole nation was suffering in the grip of the worst drought that anyone could remember. I wondered if repentance would play a part in what happened at Kansas City . . .

We had left Chicago late, and it was one-thirty in the morning before we reached Kansas City. The temperature, according to one of those digital bank signs, was 93 degrees. Even so, there was a good feeling about the city, and it wasn't just that we were relieved to have finally gotten there. Nor was it the cleanliness of the streets or the absence of any hard-looking types of either sex, hanging around or cruising the streets. It was something about the feeling of the city itself, and come to think of it, I'd noticed it before, on the one other time I had been there. The spirit of the city had a "right" feeling to it, and that was the only way to describe it.

The next four days were a whirlwind. The booksellers convention was enormous, straight-out and exciting, and when it was over, we were wrung out and exhausted. It was all we could do to shift gears and get our thinking focused on the Charismatic conference. But we had no choice; we had order forms to get printed. Wednesday, the 20th, was only six days away.

Fortunately, Pete had given us the name of a Christian printer, Larry House, and that afternoon (Friday), we called on him, to line him up. He hit us with the good news first: to help us out, he would be willing to work over the weekend, if necessary. Then came the bad news: he didn't do typesetting. We would have to bring him the announcement and order form all laid out and camera-ready. He did know of a typesetter nearby who was open till 5:30, but there was only one problem: we still didn't have the detailed information we needed to go on the announcement, and even if we did have it, we had to get someone to approve it.

We called the conference office, but by this time it was closed, and wouldn't be open until seven. It was a mandatory two-hour break, we later learned, that everyone was forced to take, otherwise too many would work right through to ten at night, without ever taking a rest. Well, we would get everything squared away over the weekend, and get the order form typeset the first thing Monday morning. If we then went straight to Larry, he should be able to have them for us by Wednesday noon. It would be tight, but barring unforeseen calamities, we should just be able to have them ready at Arrowhead by Wednesday evening.

Promptly at seven, we showed up at 1110 Grand, and rang the night bell. After a leisurely trip to the sixth floor in what had to be the pokiest elevator east of the Pecos, we stepped into a veritable bee-hive of activity. There were people manning phones, people walking briskly this way and that with important-looking papers in their hands, people briefing other people and sending them on errands — the whole thing seemed like the nerve center of some giant military operation. Yet in the midst of this activity, there was this extraordinary sense of peace — not the controlled tension that I once knew in a NORAD situation room, but genuine peace.

We introduced ourselves to the girl at the makeshift reception desk, and were soon shown into Tony Rowland's office. Tony was a Britisher by birth, in his latter forties, quiet spoken and a bit reserved. He was one of the coordinators of the People of Praise community and, we gathered, in charge of overall headquarters operations. Tony, in turn, introduced us to several others, including Bob Hagan, the office manager, who would be telling us what we needed to know about the order form.

Well, what about the order form, we asked him, without wasting any time. Bob may have been in his late forties, was gray-haired and wore glasses, and he was full of energy and bubbling humor. "We're going to need your order form by Monday morning — noon at the very latest. Fifty thousand of them. We're going to staple them together with our daily newsletter and cassette order form, and hand them out at Arrowhead, as the people come in for the first meeting, opening night."

"Monday morning!" I gasped. "You've got to be kidding! We don't even know what it's going to say yet! We might be able to make it by Wednesday noon, but that would be really pushing it."

"I'm really sorry, guys," Bob said, shaking his head, and we could see that he meant it, "but if we don't have those forms by Monday noon — I suppose you could hand them out loose," he offered.

"No," Dean said, "they'd just be thrown away. They've got to go out with the other material."

"I wish there was something I could do, but —" and Bob held out his hands, palms up.

"Thanks," I nodded, trying to smile.

Dean and I adjourned to the typing pool, which at the moment was vacated. "Well, now what?" he said, dismally.

"I don't know. Let's pray." The instant I said the words, a picture of a building flashed in my mind. I recognized the building — it would be hard to ever forget it — but it was so ridiculous, I dismissed it from my mind.

"Lord," I prayed, "we're really up against it. What do we

do now?" Immediately, the same building again came to mind. I looked up at Dean. "Well, you're not going to believe this," I said, not believing it myself, "but do you remember that big, old building we passed, walking back from the restaurant, the one with the weird sign?"

Dean nodded. It was a once-proud graystone in the business section of town, and it had an old-fashioned sign that ran the length of the building, with large tarnished brass letters deliberately set upside down:

ᵂ Ǝ S ⊥ Ǝ ᴚ N ⊥ ʎ ԀƎS Ǝ ⊥ ⊥ I N Ɔ

"Well," I said, "it's just come to mind twice. You remember what that sign said, once we'd turned it around?"

"Uh, 'Western Typesetting' —" and Dean stared at me.

"I don't know," I shrugged, "anyone so corny as —"

"That's not corny; that's smart!" Dean said, getting to his feet. We called them, they were open, and we hopped in the car and went over. It turned out that they were possibly the largest typesetter in the Midwest, and part of the service they offered was overnight typesetting. "You mean," I said to the woman behind the counter, "I can bring it in later tonight?"

"Sure, just ring the night bell."

"When will it be ready?"

"How early do you want it?"

"Eight o'clock?" I said, asking the impossible.

"It'll be ready."

Jubilant, I hurried outside to tell Dean, who was double-parked. We went back to the office, where we worked on the final text, got it approved, and returned it to Western by ten-thirty. And even though we had learned that Larry House would not be able to start printing until the following afternoon, we still requested it for eight in the morning, to give us plenty of time to make corrections.

Except that there were no corrections. It was a perfect job — the first letter-perfect piece of typesetting that I had seen during fifteen years in publishing.

If nothing else, that alone should have signaled to me that God was in charge and would shepherd our project through the valleys. I should have been rejoicing. Instead, after we'd dropped the camera-ready mechanical off at Larry's, all I could think of was all the things that could go wrong. What if he didn't have time to perforate them? What if, in all the frenetic activity of opening night, they didn't get handed out, or the committee overlooked the announcement? What if —

I felt the roller coaster we were riding had just reached the summit and was going over the top.

Since it was Sunday, the conference office would not be open until one o'clock; we decided to try the roof-top pool of the Muehlebach Hotel, where we were staying. It was a hot, still morning, but the pool was cool enough so that it didn't feel like a bathtub. As we lay there afterwards, doing nothing for practically the first time since we had left home, I got to thinking — why Kansas City? I sensed that God had picked this town for reasons other than its centrality and unusually good convention facilities.

We had gotten a clue three days before, when we had had lunch with Pete Borel, who was as quietly enthusiastic about what God was doing in his city, as he had been when I'd first met him, five years before. The local businessmen's group, "His Men", was still going strong, and there were *two* Lunch-lifts now and more than a hundred active prayer groups in the metropolitan area. And then there were the individuals, like Pete. An unassuming, indeed self-effacing, middle-aged businessman, he had nonetheless been used by the Lord as a catalyst on many occasions and seemed to have what might be called a ministry of helps. For instance, when the planning committee was looking for conference office space, he offered them two unused floors in the building his family business was in — at no cost. That, and untold incidents like it, may have had something to do with what I came to think of as the Spirit of Kansas City.

My conscience was beginning to bother me about just lying there, and so I picked up Ralph Martin's book† and started reading. I knew hardly anything about the author, other than that he was one of the original coordinators of the Word of God community, and from the way others spoke of him, I gathered that he was the Catholic Charismatic Renewal's most prophetic voice. But from just the first chapter, I felt like I knew him well — and agreed with him categorically.

His summation of the present state of society and the Church, including Charismatics, was chilling. "Concern and responsibility for other people is giving way in our society to a preoccupation with personal pleasure; serious economic problems are rousing a spirit of panicked greed. Our most basic moral institutions are threatened: family life is under serious attack; obsessive individualism is replacing community spirit . . . People in this crumbling world see a church torn in fragments by the quarrels and suspicions of hundreds of years . . . Most importantly, they see Christians whose lives fail to reflect any power or joy greater than their own. They see Christian lives, values and attitudes that are increasingly identical to those of non-Christians . . . So they turn away from Christianity and look for vitality in other directions. The message of Christianity — the judgment upon sin, the promise of salvation — goes unheard."

A crisis of global helplessness was nearing, and the author's solution? "A fundamental refounding of our lives is needed, and it must begin with radical and deep repentance and turning to God . . . 'Renewal' does express a sense of reawakened life and vitality, but it can also carry connotations of a mere revival, or modest touching up, of a structure that is basically sound. I think it is becoming clear that what Christian people need today is not just a modest

---

†*Fire on the Earth* (Word of Life, 1975)

renewal, but a far-reaching reform, involving deep repentance and radical change."

There was more in a similar vein, in this powerful exhortation which was the sort of challenge almost no one today was giving voice to. It ended on a positive note, with a brief passage from Haggai, which I had not noticed before: "Take courage, all you people of the land, says the Lord; work, for I am with you . . . My Spirit abides among you; fear not." (Hag. 2:4, 5)

The cumulative impact was such that I was not surprised that the leaders of the Catholic Charismatic Renewal had gotten together afterwards and emerged with the vision for the conference. In fact, in the wake of that message, to have done less would almost have been to refuse God's word to them.

I closed the book and my eyes, letting my mind wander again. It would be a little after one, back home. The last communicants would be coming forward in our noon service. I wondered if Fr. Lane had his traveling clothes on under his vestments. He would be heading a four-man contingent to the conference from our community, and the Winnebago would be departing as soon as the service ended. They would probably stay in New Jersey tonight, in Ohio tomorrow, in Missouri the day after . . .

Meanwhile, in Kansas City, the imminent destination of thousands of cars and campers and buses and flights, a strange lull seemed to have settled over everything. It was a sensation like standing knee-deep in a receding surf and facing the beach, with a vague awareness that an enormous breaker was gathering behind you. Everything was quiet, save for the rush of water past you, as it hastened to join that which had gone before. Soon the water level was down below your ankles, the last of it sucking at your feet as it hissed past . . .

3

The Gift of Flexibility

Entering the conference office Sunday afternoon, I was surprised to find that the peace which seemed to have settled over the city extended here as well, amplifying that which was already present. To be sure, the tempo had picked up — there were more people moving about, more requests for information being phoned in, more new workers being briefed — but a newcomer would not have guessed that the conference was now only three days away.

Tony Rowland had given us a free hand to go anywhere, talk to anyone, and ask any questions we wanted to. Since he was more or less in charge, we wanted to talk to him first. British by birth, Tony had been in America for twenty-two years, and was a citizen of this country. He was of medium build and wore a close-cropped beard that was showing signs of gray. He was Catholic, one of the four senior coordinators of the People of Praise community, and for the conference he had overall responsibility for the office, the youth and children's ministries, direction and information, health services, international guests, and press and public relations. Each of these areas had its own staff, whose managers reported to Tony, and Tony, in turn, reported to Dan De Celles, the conference director, who reported to the planning committee, in the person of its chairman, Kevin Ranaghan . . . The infrastructure was a lot more complex than I had imagined, but then, I had no idea what it took to put on a conference of this size.

Complex, yes, but surprisingly simple, I came to realize, once I had drawn up an organizational chart in my notebook, just to keep everyone straight. What it boiled down to was that every conceivable area of responsibility was covered: somewhere down the line, someone knew how many parking spaces were available at Grace and Holy Trinity Cathedral, what the best alternate routes to Arrowhead were, how many rooms were still being held in reserve at the Muehlebach, how long it would take the food service people to disburse seven thousand lunches at Municipal Auditorium . . . I chuckled, as I remembered an observation a Political Science professor had once made: the three most efficient organizations in the twentieth century were General Motors, the German General Staff, and the Catholic Church.

As Tony unfolded the layout for us, we noted that while several other communities would be providing staff-workers on many different areas, all the key managerial positions were held by members of the People of Praise community. That was only logical, since the conference was being put on by the CRS, which was itself staffed by members of the People of Praise, a number of whom had already been working on this conference for almost a year. But it had an interesting side benefit: since they had already learned how to live together in Christ, it would be much easier for them to work well together under extreme pressure, than it would be for people who were relative strangers to one another.

How were things going then? "Pretty well," Tony replied, with what I suspected was understatement. "Concerns crop up all the time, you know. We stumble across things that haven't been done, or problems arise —

but aside from solving problems and keeping things moving along, my function is to keep my people happy, in the sense of their relating to one another. If I straighten out their relationships, then the work will go well. And because that's more important than the work, my task is largely pastoral. You have to keep a sort of weather eye out for the first sign of strain."

What did he think was the most impressive thing about the conference to date? "Personally, I think it's the fact that all of these men on the planning committee, of so many different denominations, are able to get along so well. Not too many years ago, they wouldn't have given each other the time of day. Now they're working things out, really one in the Spirit, and it's a very moving thing . . .

"But I am also tremendously impressed by the way the volunteer workers have come in. They're basically working a twelve-hour day; they go home exhausted, get what sleep they can, and come back the next day. Here they are, away from home, in a strange city, working in strange surroundings, and yet, in a very short time, they have united and really started caring for one another. *That's* oneness in the Spirit! And a very touching thing . . ."

So it would seem that what the Holy Spirit was first doing here and in the planning committee could not help but have a reflection on what happens next week? "Right! Absolutely! The peace and good order that come out of these relationships will pervade the whole conference." And with that, we let Tony get back to work.

So the planning committee really was making a maximum effort to put Christ first . . . I went down the list: there was Kevin; Larry Christenson, representing the Lutheran Charismatics, Brick Bradford for the Presbyterians, Bob Hawn for the Episcopalians, Roy Lambeth for the Southern Baptists, Ken Pagard for the American Baptists, Nelson Litwiller for the Mennonites, Ross Whetstone for the Methodists, Carlton Spencer from Elim, Howard

The Gift of Flexibility

Courtney from the Foursquare Gospel Church, Vinson Synan of the Pentecostal Holiness Church, Ithiel Clemmons of the Church of God in Christ, David Stern for the Messianic Jews, and Bob Mumford and Judson Cornwall representing the nondenominationals. That was quite an assortment of individuals — if they could come together and truly be one in the Spirit, that really *was* impressive!

But, come to think of it, that was no more than Pete Borel had told us at the outset. They *wanted* it to work — badly enough to stay focused on the Lordship of Jesus and discerning His will. If that were true, then that spirit, which was similarly being manifested in the conference offices, would spread like ripples on a pond and permeate the entire conference.

As we left the conference office that afternoon, the sense of tranquillity still hung over the city. It was almost unreal, like walking through the last strains of the pastoral movement of a Beethoven symphony, and knowing what lay just a few measures ahead. But as we strolled leisurely up 12th Street, we had to remind ourselves that in three days some forty or fifty thousand people who were not here now were going to descend on this city. And most of them would be concentrated in a ten-block area from where we stood.

Sometime during the night, the roller coaster began its hurtling plummet earthwards, though at first we didn't realize it. We went down for breakfast Monday morning, hoping to get a bite to eat in the Muehlebach's coffee shop, but the waiting line was out the door. There was no time to wait; fifty thousand order forms were ready to be picked up and taken to the printer that the conference was using, to be stapled together with the newsletter and tape order form. And on top of that, we had to have six signs made up, to go in the bookstores. We checked the coffee shop at the Phillips House next door, and found the opposite problem — no customers and no waitress. Well, so much for breakfast — but on the way out, we happened to notice a sign that said conference signs were being made to order in the second floor ballroom. Dean and I looked at one another, and I pressed the up button on the elevator.

The person in charge was Vicky Huhn, from the Work of Christ community in Lansing, Michigan. At the moment, she and one helper were all that were present, though there were hundreds of poster boards stacked up and waiting, and tables with marker pens laid out on them. She assured us that thirty or so helpers would be arriving shortly, and they would be making signs all during the conference, as the requests came in. We told her our predicament, and she calmly added our request to her growing list, informing us that the signs would be delivered to the bookstores tomorrow afternoon. We thanked her — and I thanked God for once again reminding me that He was in charge.

Dean took the wagon to get the forms, while I went back to the conference office, to get as many interviews as I could, before we went out to Arrowhead in the afternoon. This time, entering the office was like walking into the newsroom of a daily paper about two hours before press time. From the typing pool came the sound of a number of typewriters going simultaneously, and there were now *two* receptionists attempting to handle incoming business calls, messages and people. At the second desk was Carmen Fraga, of the People of Praise; she looked up and smiled a greeting. It was a good feeling to know that we were now regarded as "regulars" around the office, but after having to explain to the fourth or fifth newcomer who I was and what I was doing there, I began to wish that I had a name tag like the others, or at least a Press card. And to think that I had always resented having to wear name tags!

I happened to be standing at the door of the in-

The Gift of Flexibility

formation room and could hear snatches of what the people manning the information phones were saying: "No, I'm sorry, but you can't register here; you'll have to wait till Wednesday evening, out at Arrowhead . . . You want to work for the conference? Wonderful! Report to Grace and Holy Trinity, that's the Episcopal cathedral at 13th and Broadway. They'll assign you there . . . No, I can't tell you what time the sun sets, but call back on Thursday . . ." And still, with all the commotion, there was that amazing sense of peace.

The top floor of the office building we were in had a balcony level, which meant that the conference offices actually covered a floor and a half. Up on the balcony level, people were huddled over long tables. Spying one who seemed to be momentarily alone and not on the phone, I went over. His name was Joe Stante, and he was responsible for the youth ministry. He wore a moustache, and his dark hair fell in a shock over his forehead just above his horn-rims. And the first thing he informed me was that he was not one of the full-time conference workers; he was just a school-teacher, volunteering his services.

When I learned that he was expecting nine hundred children, eleven and under, I was astonished: that was a number equal to a good-sized elementary school! What on earth would he do with them all? "Well, we've broken them down into five groups, and the two youngest — the four-to-eleven months and the one-to-two years — we're taking only in the mornings. The rest — the three-to-fives, the six-to-eights, and the nine-to-elevens — we have all day. Each group has an activity planned for it, for which we've already bought the supplies — 108 pounds of modeling clay and all that Wesson oil, twenty rubber balls, a hundred coloring books, burlap for making banners, and all that sort of thing. And then each group will spend one of those days at the zoo."

I marveled at the meticulous organization, right down to

the last detail. Was he aware of any specific instances in which God had helped them out? "The main thing that God has been doing is that He uncovers our mistakes before it's too late. For instance, whenever we order something, like how many phonographs we will need, we have nothing to go on, so all we can do is pray and ask Him to give us the number." He shrugged. "Most of the time that works out fine, but sometimes we don't hear Him right. Like, we ordered $2000 worth of snacks back at a time when we were expecting 1150 kids. Later, that projection was revised to 900, and one day, as we were going through papers and filing, something drew our attention to that particular purchase order. It was the Lord, pointing out that we didn't need as many snacks, and we were able to get the order reduced in time. That's the sort of thing the Lord does."

I thanked Joe and wished him good luck in the Lord. And only later did it occur to me that I should have asked him what the Wesson oil was for.

All at once, everyone seemed to be coming upstairs, to the open area off the balcony. "Prayer-time," somebody explained in passing. There must have been well over sixty people there, and I was able to get a seat between two new office workers, Linda Fletcher of the Servants of the Light community, and Debbie Luce, a local volunteer from the Agape youth fellowship. The meeting began with a moving, minor-key, Hebrew-type song, "The Lord is in His Holy Temple", which everyone but me seemed to know.

Dan De Celles, the conference director, reminded us to keep it down, out of consideration for the law firm, which also occupied part of the upper floors. "Make up in worship what you tone down in volume." There was some singing in the Spirit then, soft and beautiful, and in the quiet that followed, this word of prophecy came: "I give you the gift of flexibility, that you might learn to serve me in circumstances and surroundings that are unfamiliar . . .

The Gift of Flexibility 39

You must learn to move when I tell you to move, you must be peaceful in the midst of confusion . . . Know that this confusion is not of me; I give you peace."

As the meeting broke up with more worship in the Spirit, I smiled to think that if this office were indeed the nerve center of the conference, then a lot of people were going to be pleasantly surprised at the conference mood which awaited them in Kansas City.

I mentioned that to Bob Hagan, the office manager, and he laughed. "I hear you're interested in miracles," he said. "Man, they're happening all the time! Like last Sunday, a bunch of us were going to Mass, only we went to the wrong location. So we started praying about getting a cab, because we had a heavy schedule and to have to work Mass in later would have been a real hardship. The next thing you know, a car comes by and asks us if we want a lift to church." He paused. "We were very grateful, but you know, that sort of thing happens all the time around here. You couldn't put on a conference like this, without them. You take ninety volunteers like we have here, and the love just flows. The work gets put out, and we don't have big problems, because from the very first day, the relationships and our brotherhood have been the important thing."

Dean had returned and came up to join us. "No, I'm really grateful," Bob continued. "I've seen God work some great miracles in my life. My wife and I were in Florida two years ago, praying at a shrine, when God revealed to me that He was going to give us a son, and I was to name him Isaac. Well, I told my wife, she just laughed, because it had been twenty years since she had been pregnant and was long past the time when she could have a child. Nevertheless, we asked the Lord for a passage from Scripture, specifically the story of Abraham and Sarah. My wife said, 'I'm going to make sure I open to the Old Testament,' only she didn't notice that she was holding the Bible upside down. She opened to the New Testament — to

Hebrews 11, where Paul tells of the faith of Abraham and Sarah."

Someone called to Bob, about a problem with one of the typewriters, and he said he'd be right there. "The following February, she was very ill, and it turned out she was pregnant. The doctors said it was going to be a retarded child, and that she would have great problems with the pregnancy, but she went through that nine months with no further problems at all. Then, when the actual time came for her to deliver, the baby wouldn't come. So we prayed for, oh, maybe an hour, and the baby started coming so quickly that they could barely get her into the delivery room in time." Bob got up and started toward the typing pool.

"Hey, Bob!" I called after him. "Wait a minute! What happened?"

"Oh," he said, turning back with a grin, "he was a fine, healthy boy. Name of Isaac. Eight months old now. He's here at the conference," he said with a twinkle in his eye, as he descended the staircase, "maybe you'll meet him later." (We did, the following afternoon, when Bob's wife brought him into the office. And that was the second time I saw Dean moved to tears.)

Our next stop was Jim Harcus's office. Jim was a tall burly Scot, with a thick accent, who was in charge of finances and budget. He and his family had been members of the People of Praise for two and a half years, before which he had been an officer in a large international corporation with personal responsibility for nine plants throughout America and overseas. I told him that Kevin had revealed to us their projected deficit of a quarter of a million dollars — what were they going to do about it?

"We're going to advise the Body of Christ at Arrowhead of our exact financial situation and allow them to respond to the best of their ability," he replied simply. And he went on to explain that they were keeping a daily watch on all their accounts, so that the planning committee

The Gift of Flexibility 41

could have the latest bottom-line figure, whenever they needed it. I was amazed at how calm he appeared, and we learned that he had had to completely re-learn his whole approach to his own field of expertise. For instance, when the registrations began coming in way behind their projection, and it looked like their deficit was going to be overwhelming, Jim's initial reaction was to respond to the curves with strong corrective action. Instead, he was repeatedly told: "Have no fear; the Lord will take care of it." And they just transmitted their concerns to prayer groups who passed them on to other prayer groups.

"In the last week before the deadline for registration, we expected to receive fifteen percent of our total registration. Suddenly there was a surge, and we received more like twenty-five per cent! And what's more, there's now a sizable category of voluntary donations, where people have sent in gifts of twenty, fifty, and even a hundred dollars, saying 'I can't attend, but please accept this.'" Jim turned his broad hands, palms up. "So, I am learning."

We still had almost an hour before we were due to leave for Arrowhead, so we talked next to Joe Heintzelman. After two days of trying to talk to him, we found a moment when his phone was uncharacteristically silent, and made the most of the opportunity. Soft-spoken and in his twenties, Joe had thinning blond hair and a thick beard to match. A comparatively old hand at large conferences, he was one of the growing number that I was coming to think of as the "young unflappables" — cool, poised, and almost clinically competent. It was somewhat disconcerting to stop and realize that practically everyone in a key managerial position was under forty (especially when one had just turned forty oneself).

Joe had overall responsibility for: facilities (all the conference and workshop sites), the three bookstores, the taping, the display show (some sixty booths around the perimeter of the main bookstore in the lower level of the old municipal auditorium), the food service, and the logistics. How were things going? "Well, you always expect *some* confusion around now, things you hadn't anticipated."

Then he would be here, trouble-shooting, during the conference? Getting things straightened out by phone? "No, I'll be on the move, making the rounds. But I'll still be in touch," and he held up a shiny piece of electronic equipment that clipped on his belt. "It's called a belt-beeper."

I was skeptical. "How does the thing work?"

"Well, a person calls my number, which calls the belt-beeper. They have twelve seconds to give a message, which comes right over the beeper."

"You mean, it's sort of a one-way walkie-talkie?"

"Right. There's no way I can respond back to them, but if they say, 'Joe, call so-and-so at the Trade Mart,' I can get to the nearest phone and make contact." He looked at the metallic object in his hand. "This is the first time we've ever used them. They're pretty expensive, but we've never been this spread out before . . ."

"Do you feel like you're stretched too thin?" I asked, watching his face closely.

"No," he said resolutely, "because we're working with facilities that are very professional and experienced in dealing with conferences. And so I figure with the Lord's help and all the brothers we have around, we can handle just about any problem that comes up."

Joe had mentioned food service — what exactly did that entail? "Getting seventeen thousand lunches to seventeen thousand people in several different locations precisely at noon," he smiled. "Suppers, too. That's how many people bought meal tickets with their registrations."

The mind reeled at the thought. And what was 'logistics' all about? "Well, first there's the labor pool — a bunch of volunteers who are asked to stand by until they're needed. Then if one of my facility managers suddenly discovers that

The Gift of Flexibility

a workshop which is supposed to have 350 chairs set up, has been overlooked, we can dispatch a dozen workers from the labor pool to go out there and take care of that. And then there's parking and transporting speakers and the like out to Arrowhead and the different other sites. We'll have fifteen cars just for that purpose."

How many of his managers and key personnel were from the People of Praise? "About 90%."

I was struck again by the fact that so many of the people in crucial positions already knew one another, indeed were covenanted together as members of the same family in Christ. Joe smiled. "Our lifestyle in the community is just carried over into our working environment," he summed up.

We had time for one more interview, but since no one seemed to be relatively free, we went and sat in the typing pool which was quiet for the time being — all fourteen machines and three transcribers were unoccupied. It was good to just sit down and be silent for a moment — for the first time all day, I realized. I glanced idly around the typing pool. It was hardly elegant — the typewriters were rented machines, set out on long utility tables with rented chairs in front of them. But on the tables was an ample supply of copy paper, pens, pencils, stationery, envelopes, paper clips, Correcto-type, phone books, and someone had even thought to put out one of those handy little blue word-spellers — incredible! "Loving" was the word to describe the care that had gone into the smallest detail.

Nan Jenkins, the assistant office manager, poked her head around the corner about then, and so we asked her if she would care to join us for a minute. Friday night, while we were readying our order form, we'd noticed her come in with another worker and pray that the Lord would reveal to them the whereabouts of a lost memo — had He done so? She laughed and shook her head. "Sorry to spoil a story, but we never did find that file." She pursed her lips.

"Something interesting did happen, though. That memo was one of several important ones that Dan De Celles had asked to have typed, and to lose something like that, I expected to be in really hot water. I mean, people were already looking through the trash. But when I went to tell Dan, all he said was, 'Don't worry about it; the Lord will take care of it. If it's that urgent, the person to whom it was addressed will come back and ask the question again.' I was really shocked," she said, her eyes wide. "And very grateful."

Had God given her any direct assistance that she was aware of? "I think that the outstanding thing in the ten days that I've been here, has been that every time I needed something done, or had counted on someone who hadn't shown up, someone else would walk in the door and say, 'No one's ever called me to work, but can I do something?' If we needed a typist, it would turn out that she was a typist; if it was a package to be delivered, it would be a guy who could make the delivery."

She looked at Dean and me. "I've just graduated from college, and this is my first job. You know what? I think I have this job because the Lord wants to teach me a lot of things about trusting Him."

I didn't say anything, but I had the feeling that if I really listened, I just might hear a still, small voice telling me the same thing.

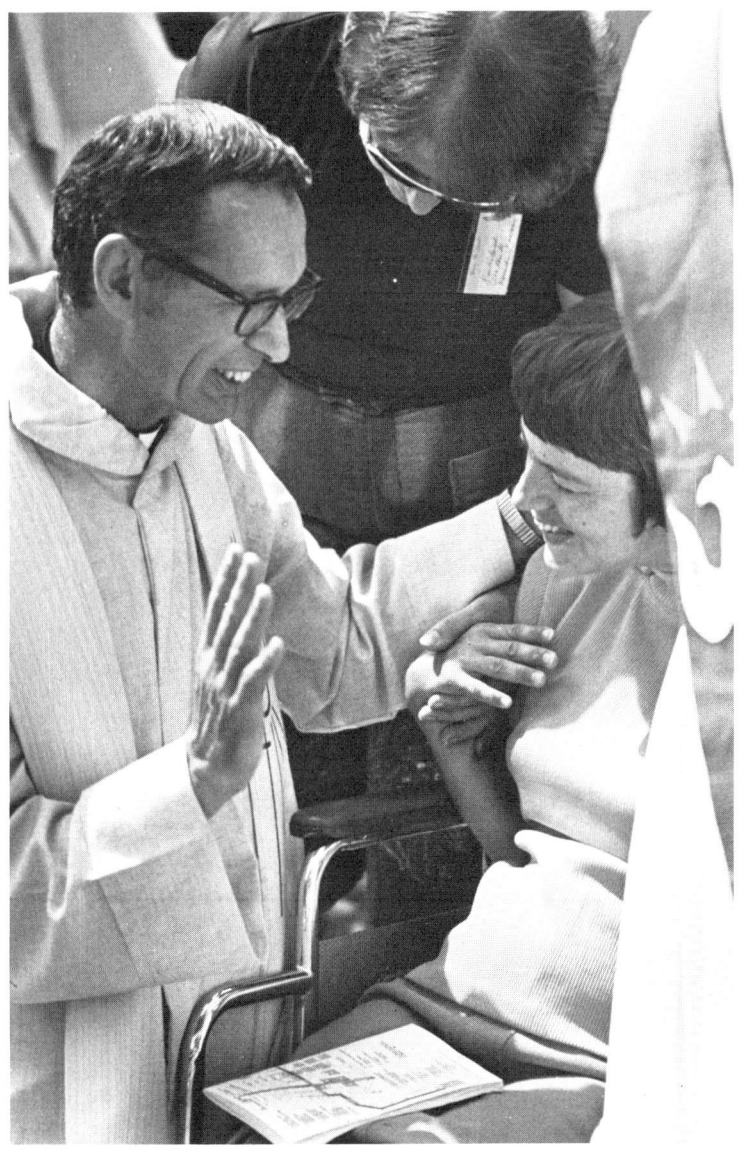

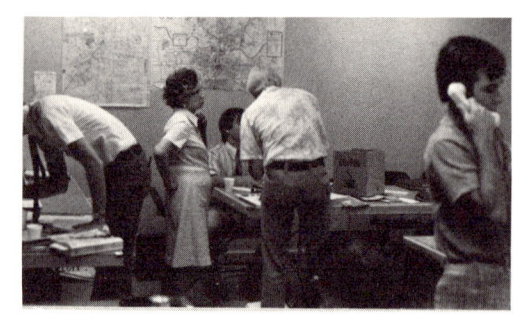

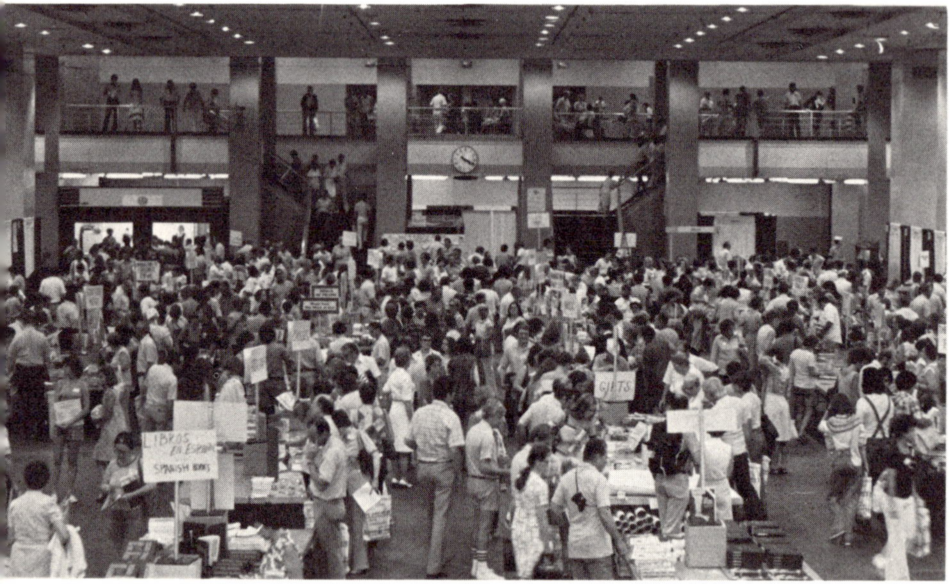
LIBROS
SPANISH BOOKS
GIFTS

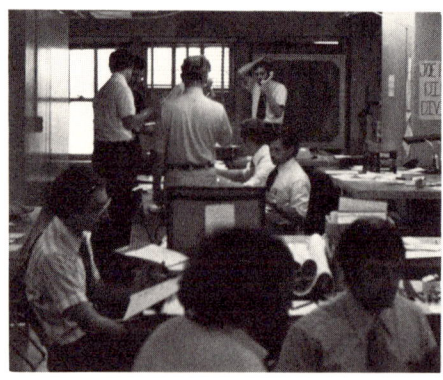

Mike Evans

Marjorie and Brick Bradford

David and Martha Stern

4

Riding the Elephant

Even with the temperature a broiling 98 degrees, it was a relief to get out of the office and get into the wagon, en route for Arrowhead. My mind was so full of impressions and information that it felt like a bowl piled high with slippery spaghetti that I was gingerly carrying to the table. One jostle, and half of it would slither out of the bowl and onto the floor.

We rode in silence, listening to the gentle noise of the air-conditioner and trying to assimilate the events of the morning. For ten minutes or so, we watched the shimmering scenery along I-70. "That's 435 coming up," I murmured to Dean, who was driving. "Watch for the Blue Ridge cutoff. We want parking area E." I yawned. "Boy, I'm beat. Completely walked and talked out."

Dean nodded. "Me, too." I was going to suggest that we take a break and get some lunch, but we were way away from anywhere — and just then we came to our exit, and I had to navigate us past the baseball stadium, also new, and back around behind the football stadium. The two stadiums together were breathtaking — clean and modern, they sat in the middle of an endless apron of asphalt that looked like it could handle all the cars in Kansas City. We found Gate E without too much trouble and took the elevator to the press room on the fourth floor.

Paneled in dark wood, and with wood and red leather booths, soft indirect lighting, a plush red carpet and a long, dark oak bar, the press room looked like Anheuser-Busch's idea of what every drinking man wished his neighborhood pub looked like. I noted that the shelves behind the bar were empty and was glad to see that liquor would not be served, even though there would be a number of secular press present. At the entrance, two men were erecting a series of mail slots for the different papers and publications, and after a little looking, we found ours.

"You know," I confessed to Dean, "for years I've been going to stadiums, and I've always wondered what a press room looked like. I used to think of it as an elite place, much more so than the owner's box, or whatever. Like you had to belong to a secret society to get in. Now we're here, and legitimately." But Dean was unimpressed and asked a girl manning the phone where we could find Ronn Kerr, the man in charge of the press room. I asked another girl for our press credentials, and even that was something special. In college, when I had realized that writing was what I wanted to do more than anything else, the best newspaper writing was being done on the sports pages. I used to imagine myself with an old hat on the back of my head (with the obligatory press pass stuck in the band, of course), tapping out the next morning's lead story on an old Royal.

"Hi! I'm Jo Kerr, Ronn's wife. He's tied up at the moment, but he'll be with you as soon as he can. You're the ones doing the book, aren't you? Are you all set?"

"We'll need two other sets of credentials," Dean answered, "for Carol Showalter and John Sorensen."

Carol's husband Bill was pastor of the Parkminster Presbyterian Church in Rochester, New York, and they were conducting one of the workshops together, on Christian marriage. They were good friends, and Carol had written a book that we would be publishing shortly. John, a good photographer, was one of the four men coming from our community. "We may have a few other helpers," I added, "who won't need full press credentials —"

"No problem," said Jo, "give us their names, when you have them, and we will issue them press room volunteer passes." She straightened and smiled. "Would you like to see the press box?"

We nodded and followed her through a small, oak-paneled door. The visual impact took my breath away. There, beyond ten-foot, plate glass windows, was the most modern stadium I had ever seen. There were three tiers of seats, in bold orange, yellow, and burgundy, and the field was emerald green. So intense was the noonday sun that the colors were dazzling, almost too bright to look at. And then I noticed the silence; it was so quiet, it was like being in a sound studio. "Oh, wow," I whispered.

Jo remembered something and excused herself for a moment. We were standing at one end of the press box which extended from thirty-yard-line to thirty-yard-line. There were three levels of desks which were actually long, white formica counters, with plush, leather-padded swivel chairs in front of each place, well over a hundred in all. On the top level, typewriters stretched from one end to the other.

I felt like a kid at Christmas! Dean looked over at me, and seeing the expression on my face, nodded in the direction of the typewriters. "Why don't you try one out?"

"Nah," I said, trying to sound as if I meant it, and beginning to feel really foolish.

"Go ahead," Dean said, straight-faced, "put down your first impressions." So I shrugged like it was no big deal, sat down at the first typewriter (an IBM, not a Royal), turned it on, and stared at it.

Dean raised his eyebrows. "No paper," I explained sheepishly. He tore a piece from his note pad and gave it to me. I cranked it in, looked out at the field and started to type (three fingers, not two):

"The press box is so heavily soundproofed, it makes everything unreal, as if the stadium itself is holding its breath. There's no wind, so it must be well over a hundred down on the field. A couple of men are working out there, up on the speakers' platform, erecting some sort of overhead framework. They're moving slowly, to conserve energy in the extreme heat. The artificial turf has sheets of plywood covering it, making a road out to the platform, to protect it from the pick-up truck that the men have brought their materials in. Over in the east end zone, there are two little boys who couldn't be more than seven or eight, running make-believe pass patterns. They seem oblivious to the heat, that's how much of a thrill it is to be playing on the same field that their heroes play on.

"I can't get over how eerie this air-conditioned silence is. Is *this* the real world, or is that, out there? Come Wednesday night, this place will be alive with activity, but now, looking out at that splash of vibrant color, and listening to the silence..." I tore the sheet out and handed it to Dean, who looked at it noncommitally and tucked it away.

Jo returned then and told us a little bit about Ronn's background. We learned that he had been in advertising and quit to go to Methodist seminary and become ordained, some ten years ago. He had been increasingly involved in Christian communications, and now he had formed this association, "a non-profit public foundation, chartered to provide services to institutions involved in Christian ministry."

The door opened, and Ronn joined us. He was soft-spoken, with rimless glasses and thinning hair, and I wondered what was the biggest technical problem he faced at the moment? "When we were here three months ago to check the place out, we were elated. It was superbly equipped. Everyone overlooked the fact that the week before the conference, the Chiefs went into pre-season training camp. They took all their telecopiers and darkroom equipment with them, and right now, our photographer is calling all over town to locate an enlarger and a film processor. But we'll get it worked out."

What kind of press response was he getting? "We're really excited about the way things are shaping up. For one thing, the press corps that's coming is on a much higher level than anything I've been associated with. It looks like we're going to run 250 to 275 registered press, and well over half of them are from secular media. NBC Nightly News is coming, and both wire services are sending their national men from New York. The New York *Times* is coming, the Washington *Post*, the Los Angeles *Times*, the Boston *Globe*, two Chicago papers — if you were to put together a list of the fifty biggest daily papers that you would want to cover an event, they'll all be here. And French national television will be represented; there's even a reporter coming from Australia. In fact, with the exception of the Congress of Evangelism, which the Billy Graham organization sponsored in Lausanne in '73, from a press standpoint this is probably the biggest worldwide religious event in a couple of decades."

What was attracting the press in such numbers? "One thing, of course, is Ruth Stapleton, who is much more newsworthy, now that her brother is President. But from the pre-conference questions we've been getting, I would say that the most interest is in the ecumenical flavor of the thing. The old hands are aware of the ecumenical movements of the Fifties and Sixties, which lost most of their original impetus. But those were generated by what might be labeled the liberal, social-action oriented segment of the Church, and the Charismatic Renewal defies conventional definition. What's more, this conference will be demonstrating a much broader ecumenism than the earlier sponsored versions, and this is what a lot of the secular press is picking up."

We thanked Ronn, and told him we'd see him tomorrow

afternoon, when we were scheduled to follow him with a brief presentation to the planning committee. The drive back to town took seventeen minutes, a fact I filed away for future reference. By the time we got the wagon parked, it was after five, which meant the conference office would be closed for two hours. "I vote we go up to the room and have a soda and lie down," Dean said, clapping his hands together, as if it were already settled.

I looked at him askance. "You know perfectly well that if we do, you'll take your shoes off. And once you've taken your shoes off, it's 'game over' — there'll be no getting you up again. Why don't we go out and have a good dinner, instead? We haven't eaten all day."

"Man, I'm too tired to appreciate it." So we compromised and went up to the room for half an hour before going out, and Dean kept his shoes on.

Back in the conference office, a little after seven, we were able to find a quiet moment with the conference director, Dan De Celles. At twenty-seven, Dan was calm and cheerful, and always seemed to have a minute for someone who needed to talk to him. A Notre Dame graduate, he was one of the newer coordinators of the People of Praise community. His uncle, Paul De Celles, was a professor at Notre Dame, and the overall coordinator for the People of Praise. Dan and his wife were responsible for one of the community's extended households — two children, plus four single women and three guys. This was his third major conference; he had been assistant to the director at the '74 Notre Dame conference, then director at the regional conference in Detroit, and director for the last Notre Dame conference.

Was there anything significantly different about this one? "This one is phenomenally different from what we're used to. One, it's a new city with entirely new facilities and six hundred miles away from home base. And we're not starting off small and just adding to an existing conference structure, refining it and making it better, as at Notre

Dame. We're starting off huge, and we're starting from scratch. Also, at Notre Dame, it was basically one group you were working with, and our speakers knew what to expect. Here, we're dealing with a lot of different folks we've never worked with before and how they would like to do things, and so you have an awful lot of exceptions, and that takes time."

He looked as though he were bearing up pretty well, all things considered, and one gathered that he liked his work. Dan laughed, "Conferences are wild! You start with a staff of four or five and wind up with over a thousand before you're done. And the vast majority have never done it before! Yet these are the very ones whose cooperativeness and brotherhood you have to rely on. In the final month before the conference, everyone's dedication and willingness to work is really something! They don't know what they're doing, but they jump right in and learn what to do as they go." He laughed again. "Putting on a conference is like riding an elephant. At first, it's just walking along, and you're holding the ears, and you can steer it which way you want it to go very easily. Then it picks up some speed, and it's loping along, but you can still control it, you know. But finally, when it gets to galloping, you find that all you can do is hang on for dear life! And this one reached the galloping stage three months ago! Thundering through the jungle —" And we all roared with laughter.

We had one more division director to see that evening — Adrian Reimers, who was dressed like a young businessman and gave an impression of precision and efficiency, which was further borne out when we asked him what he did. "My responsibility is registration, housing, personnel, and the official program. Briefly, the housing is being handled through the convention and visitors bureau here in Kansas City. They're processing between ten and thirteen thousand requests for rooms, and housing for somewhere between twenty-five and thirty thousand people. The preregistration, as you know, was done in South Bend. It was a unique experience for us, the first time we've ever gone onto a computer."

Had they purchased this service from somebody? "No, that was one of the things the Lord did for us. We had toyed with the idea of computerized registration for a long time, because it's such a big headache, with monstrous files all over the place. And Notre Dame would let us use their computer at a very reasonable rate. But the big problem was: where do you get the software for it?"

"What's software?"

"The program — how you process the stuff. So, just as we were considering going to a software house, to have a program custom-made for us, a young man named John Annable came to our community, unemployed. He just happened to be a computer programmer, so he put the program together for us. In fact, he did a very good job for us and had it ready to run when we were ready to start producing."

Where was Adrian running into his biggest problem now? "For some reason, it's all in the area of the guest speakers — communicating with them, keeping track of their accounts, and particularly getting them housed. Just in the past day, we've run into a bunch of problems with reservations made for people, and which the Muehlebach does not seem to have data on. My personal opinion is that it's the work of the Devil."

That witnessed to us, because the Muehlebach had done a beautiful job of organizing the CBA, just the week before. I suggested that, with all the other areas going so smoothly, it would be just like the Old Boy to do all he could to sour new arrivals on the way the conference was being run. What better way to turn a speaker off on the CRS, than to have him come in from out of town, tired and looking forward to a day or two of quiet before the conference begins, and find that he's being put in a room in which someone else is already ensconced.

Adrian looked at me, his head cocked. "Did you know that that has already happened?" And he mentioned the name of a well-known speaker to whom that had happened that very morning.

What about personnel? "We've had to recruit fifteen hundred workers, which is at least twice as many as we've ever had working on a conference before." Did that mean that they would have to reach way beyond the normal labor reserves in their fellow communities? "That's right. Here in town, Agape and the people from Broadway Baptist have been very, very helpful. And then, other communities and fellowships are helping out, too." He leaned back at his desk. "All things considered, this conference is going into the final hours of preparation remarkably smoothly. I cut my teeth on the Rome conference in '75. *That* one was something else!"

I smiled. "Did you learn a little Italian?" I asked, imagining the difficulties he must have run into.

"I didn't learn a whole lot of Italian," and he winced at the memory. "I learned basically that you cannot have a large conference in Rome! I think we all learned that. That whole conference was a miracle!" he said ruefully, and we all laughed. "No, this one, for all its size and complexity, is much more orderly. I've even brought my wife along, and she's due to have a baby in two and a half weeks."

It was nearly ten, the time the office closed. We thanked Adrian and headed up to the Muehlebach. Walking up the steep street, I noted that the temperature had fallen to 94 degrees, though the humidity was still high. "Do I feel sorry for those coming to the conference, who won't be able to sleep where it's air-conditioned!" I said to Dean.

"Sleep!" he exclaimed, like a character out of Dickens, "Have you not learned, my boy, that Charismatics never sleep? They'll be so busy sharing their blessings that they'll forget all about sleep, *and* the humidity."

But I still thanked God that we were able to go into our clammy cool room and collapse.

5

In the Submarine

Tuesday morning dawned much too early — at about seven-thirty, the sun figured out how to get through the curtains, and it was time to get going. Once again, the coffee shop downstairs was too crowded, so we decided to skip breakfast. Dean was going to take the wagon, to drop off some order forms at the conference bookstores, while I went directly to the office, to get the rest of the pre-conference story. But on the way, as I walked down 12th, I realized I was hungrier than I had thought.

At that moment, I passed a red neon sign at eye level — "cafeteria" — and looking up, I saw that it was in the lower level of a Kresge's. On an impulse, I went in. There was hardly anyone there, and so a couple of minutes later, I was sitting in a booth, about to enjoy scrambled eggs and juice, when a voice behind me said, "All right, hold it!" I froze, turned around, and there was Dean grinning broadly. "You forgot to give me the car keys."

"How'd you know where to find me?"

"I didn't. I went to the office, and they hadn't seen you, so I just said, 'Well, Lord, you know where he is; I sure don't,' and started walking. This was the first place I got a nudge to look." And so we had breakfast together.

In the Submarine

Once in the office, one seemed to lose all sense of time. With no windows, there was no quick visual reference to what time of the day or night it was, and since the pressure was consistent, the days of the week seemed to blur together. Yet along with the pressure, there was again this uncanny sense of peace. I noticed Pat Desmond pouring himself a cup of coffee, so I asked him about it. "I think it has a lot to do with the half-hour prayer meeting we have every morning. That really sets the tone for the whole day. And the basic idea of putting brotherhood before the job — to do that, we have to be constantly aware of the need for forgiveness and reconciliation. That's something we've learned in community and are applying here. And it works! It's such a radical departure from standard business practice that I've often thought, if I were a business major going for an MBA, I'd want to do a study on it. Because from a business point of view, the results are phenomenal."

At that moment, Pat was concerned about lining up forty thousand communion wafers for the Catholic Masses, and eight thousand for the Episcopalians, so I let him go. I talked next with Paul Barrett, a strong, quiet young man who was in charge of all the conference and workshop facilities. Part of his responsibility was security — ensuring that there were no disruptions at any of the sessions, and especially at Arrowhead. I asked him if there had ever been such an instance.

"Once, I think it was three years ago, some crazy guy ran out on the field and tried to plant some weird symbol in front of the speakers' platform. The point is, he could have as easily run up on the platform and smacked someone. Ever since then, we've been a lot more conscious of the need to provide some sort of protection against that sort of thing."

Could he give any specific examples of where the Lord had directly aided him in his work? "Well, just the fact that I have my sanity right now," he chuckled. "Because I've never done anything like this before and never wanted to. But I love it now, though I know how true it is, what Paul De Celles, the overall coordinator of our community said, that a lot of those working on the conference would be operating on just the strength the Lord had given them. I know I'm one of those. I can't do this. And it's very clear to me that I can't. But the encouraging thing is, it's also very clear to me that the Lord has His hand on my life. I can face things with less fear and trembling, because He's been faithful up to this point." I smiled. "In myself, I can't do what I'm expected to do tomorrow. But then, I haven't been able to do what I'm expected to do today, either. So I might as well just not worry about it and trust the Lord."

The planning committee was running a little late that afternoon. With so much happening now, not even the most resilient agenda could be adhered to. Dean and I were standing in the hall outside the conference room, waiting for Ronn Kerr to finish his presentation. When he was done and came out, there were a few minutes before we would be called. Ronn whispered to us: "Did you hear? We got the enlarger and the processor!"

"No kidding, how?"

"The enlarger isn't that much of a story — we finally found one we could rent — but the processor is interesting, because we'd called all over town, and there wasn't one to be had anywhere. By mid-morning we'd run out of time, because we had to have prints ready, to test-run photographs on the big, computerized scoreboard out there. So I said to our photographer, 'All right, let's call it. We'll have to buy a bunch of trays and go through tray processing.' Just then, Jo was registering the reporter from the paper over in Raytown. He's an ex-missionary who didn't find a church situation and so was teaching journalism at the high school and doing some stories for the paper.

"Anyway, he overheard our predicament and said, 'Excuse me, but we have a new automatic processor in the high school darkroom. The school's closed for the summer — let me see what I can do.' A little later he called up: 'It's all set, I'm going to clean it up, and I'll bring it over this afternoon.' Isn't that something?"

"Praise God!" we whispered.

The door opened, and we were invited in. Kevin was at the end of a long table, at which there were a few vacant seats. There were still some familiar faces, though — Judson Cornwall, whose first book I had edited . . . Brick Bradford . . . Vinson Synan . . . We took five minutes to explain what we were doing, after which they asked a few pertinent questions, expressed their approval and that was it. Not nearly as demanding as I had anticipated. Dean, as usual, had been completely unperturbed. The only thing that seemed to move him in Kansas City was the deep and beautiful working of God, and it was becoming less and less unusual to see his eyes brim with emotion. The grizzled, weather-beaten exterior was only an exterior, after all.

Back in the office that evening, it was as if we had never left. The same tempo, the same pressure — the same peace. But now some tell-tale signs of strain were beginning to show up. There was a cot up on the balcony level, out of the main traffic flow, for anyone to lie down on and rest, and it was in almost constant use. And there were circles under a number of eyes, others were bloodshot, and people were having to make a conscious effort to remember things.

Waiting for Dan De Celles to approve our suggested

announcement for opening night, we talked with his assistant, Caron Olson. Among other things, she happened to mention that one of the difficult parts of her job was what to say, when people came in who were quite certain that God had told them that they were to serve in a special capacity or to provide music for the conference. Their motives were unquestionably sincere; and so how did one tell them that until God told the planning committee the same thing — ?

Dan waved us in, and we were glad we didn't have to answer that one. Afterwards, we talked to Steve Hilker, one of the few department managers who was not a member of the People of Praise. Steve was responsible for Direction & Information, and a member of the Work of Christ community, which was concentrating its efforts in this particular area. Stocky and sporting a large red beard, Steve was in his twenties, and at the moment he was working with three girls on his staff who openly eavesdropped on our conversation and made only half-hearted attempts to stifle their laughter when something we said amused them.

As of right then, how many signs had his team made up? "About two thousand. Turned out by nearly a hundred workers, including a fair number from Agape."

Were any of them professional sign-makers before? "It's a gift of the Holy Spirit," Steve responded with a straight face, to the muffled delight of his co-workers.

What would he say was his biggest problem? "Uh . . . who?"

"No names, please."

The phone rang, and Steve, much relieved, answered it. When he finished, he told us that his biggest problem was that he had had barely five weeks to get his team organized. He gave us a glimpse of his working notebook which contained, among other things, an organizational chart that would have done justice to a major corporation. Something else caught my eye — part of a memo to information-booth workers, which I asked if I might copy:

> II. Relating to conference participants
>   A. Minister the Lord's love.
>   B. Remain calm, focus on the Lord.
>   C. Have a servant's heart
>   — You should desire to serve the participants more than yourself, and you'll need the Lord's help to do this.
>   D. Speak clearly
>   — Don't assume people know what you are talking about.

"You know," said Steve, "it would cost six or seven times as much to put a conference like this on in the world, because you'd have to pay so much for the work that's being done here by volunteers. These people are knocking themselves out, and they're not being paid anything. Like yesterday: we needed some transportation input in a hurry, so I delegated the job to a girl: 'Find out everything you can about everything that moves in this city.' Within two hours, she had a list of all the taxi cab places, their phone numbers, and the areas they served; local bus information, including a large box full of maps and schedules; the long-distance buses, like Continental and Greyhound, and their departure schedules; a complete list of the airport limousine services, with an express system that the airport had set up to service the motels; the railroad schedules, and numbers people could call for arrival and departure information — I mean, it was incredible!"

We concurred, and as it was getting near closing time, we said good night and waved goodbye to Carmen, who had been on one of the reception desks since eight that morning. Just as we were going out the door, out of the corner of my eye I saw a young fellow coming downstairs who looked like he wanted to talk to us. This was David Grimm, a volunteer from the Lamb of God community. "Something happened this afternoon that I thought you might be interested in. The thought came to me that I ought to make myself available to pick people up, so I did, and was told that a Fr. Bennett had said he would be flying in to the municipal airport in a Beechcraft and would appreciate a lift. They couldn't be sure if anyone had been sent or not, but I went anyway. What I didn't realize was how difficult that old airport is to figure out. I asked a guy who worked out there, and he said, 'Well, he could be coming in at . . .' and he named one of the buildings. 'Or it could be . . .' There were five, all told. One was Executive Beechcraft, so I took a chance that that might be the one.

"I drove about two miles around the whole airport to this building, and when I inquired inside, the lady at the counter said, 'We have no record of who's coming in or going out of here.' I called back to the office, but they still didn't have anything definite, though they were going to try to find out and call me back. But after waiting a few minutes, I started to leave, when a priest came walking in the door. 'Are you Fr. Bennett?' I asked, and he said, 'Yes, praise the Lord.' Just then, the phone rang. I answered it and said, 'Never mind, I found him, and his wife is with him.' Anyway," David concluded, "I thought you might be interested."

We thanked him for the story and left. That night, or rather, the following morning, I had a just-before-waking dream, so vivid that I knew I would be able to remember it, without writing it down. I was in a forest, and it was dusk, almost night. I could barely see what was around me. Walking forward slowly, I felt a tremendous peace, so strong that it was like love, and so tender that I felt close to tears.

Ahead in the dim light, I discerned different species of animals, lying on what looked like low, slatted wood platforms under the low-hanging boughs of trees. There was a rabbit and a squirrel and a young deer and some birds . . . as they watched me approach, I could see that they were clearly apprehensive. But they didn't bolt. They lay still, almost trembling. I even reached out and touched the flank of the deer. He gave a start, but he did not spring up and bound away.

Then a voice behind me said, "They trust you, because I am here. I want you to learn to trust me, as they do. When you do, they will trust you, too." And then I woke up. I mentioned it to Dean, when we said a prayer before going down, but with the press of ensuing events, it was soon forgotten.

Ten hours after we'd left the conference office, we were back in it again. And so was everyone else. There was a certain bond between us now, like we were a submarine crew that had been submerged at sea for many days together. We knew the inside of the hull by memory, and we were comfortable with one another. To be sure, we would have liked to surface, however briefly, for some fresh air and sunshine, but we knew we were doing what had to be done, and we had learned patience. Meanwhile, the sub glided on silently towards its destination . . . .

There were four more people on our list, and then our work in the office would be finished. The first was Mary Lou Bradley, in charge of health arrangements. From her we learned that they were readying first aid stations to serve anywhere from forty to sixty thousand people, and that out at Arrowhead, there would be eight mobile teams, ready to respond immediately to any trouble. Thanks to the Red Cross, and a minor miracle, they would have an extremely efficient method of signaling for help.

"When I got to town two days ago," Mary Lou said,

"the first thing I did was check in with the Red Cross, and they asked me if we had any system for the ushers to flag for help. Well, we thought we had planned for every contingency, but that one we hadn't. We were told that what we needed were two-foot-square flags on short sticks — one for each aisle usher. There were seventy-five aisle ushers! By 'coincidence,' the three girls who had ridden with me from South Bend were not yet committed to a specific work assignment, so guess what they've been doing every minute since they arrived? Right! By seven tonight, the last orange flag will be stapled to the last short stick!"

We laughed and thanked Mary Lou. It was ten o'clock on Wednesday morning — D-Day, I realized with a start — and the busiest place in the office was the desk of John Grcich. ("That's right," Joe Heintzelman had assured us, "that's the way it's spelled. But everyone who sees it spelled that way, wants to correct it. It's pronounced Gursich.") John was on the phone, and his assistant, sitting next to him, was also on the phone. There were two people standing in front of John's desk, waiting to speak to him the moment he got off the phone, and on top of that, his belt-beeper, lying on the desk top, was beeping. For awhile we just stood out of the way and watched this blond young man handle one crisis after another, never losing his equanimity.

But as with so many of the others, what initially appeared to be supreme self-confidence, turned out to be simple trust, when there finally came enough of a lull to talk to John. "What I'm finding is that I've got so much on my mind, I can't remember it all. I'll initiate some work on a project, and then I'll forget to follow up on it, and then, when they come back to me, I'll find that a great deal of work has been done on it. And there seems to be no one there who's done the work." He looked up at us. "And then there's more conventional ways that He helps us, too. Like yesterday: we had a four-page parking plan that had to be gotten out this morning, which meant that it had to be to the printer no later than one, yesterday afternoon. When I turned it in to the printer at four-thirty, he said there was no way. Yet somehow, he had 185 copies for me twenty-five minutes later!"

It was now ten-fifteen, and the noise and activity level had reached a peak. I was standing next to Ralph Rath, of the People of Praise, who was formerly a reporter on the Oakland *Tribune*, and was now working with Ronn Kerr's organization. How did the whole thing feel to him right now? "Frankly, it's a little confusing at the moment, with so many things breaking at once. But if we've done our preparation right, we see it all work out in the end . . . It's easier to see back in South Bend. When one area looked like, logically, it was going to fail, we'd just turn it over to the Lord in prayer." He laughed. "Judging from the feel of things around here, I'd say we could use some prayer right now." And almost as if that were a cue, people started assembling chairs on the upper level for prayer time.

The last person we talked to in the office was Brian Gaffney, a moustached young man with a perpetual smile who was in charge of programming, a loose category covering all arrangements with speakers. He told us that they had had a good meeting with the Muehlebach's staff. What had been happening was that speakers were arriving a day or two later than they had originally intended, and their reservations were going into the 'no-show' category. It had all gotten ironed out, and the hotel was actually grateful to have the conference people looking over their shoulder, as it were.

"The reason they haven't given us a hard time," Brian said, "is that we didn't start yelling at them, saying 'You blew it for us, and we want you to fix it!' They said that if we had come on like that, they would have told us, 'You can go scratch.' I never lost my cool at the hotel, and neither have any of my people. What we do is explain,

'We've got a problem; can we work it out somehow?' "

I was led to ask Brian how old he was; twenty-two, he replied.

Our tour in the submarine was up at last. After nearly six days, Dean and I were about to surface. As Dean went to check our message box for the last time, I waited by the bulletin board and jotted down some of the announcements I found posted there:

> Men and women working in the office should dress in a way that gives honor and glory to our God! For men, that means a shirt and tie; women should dress in a way that is neat, attractive and modest . . .
>
> We share this building with many others, and we need to be the best of stewards. Let's keep treating everyone in the building with as much love and consideration as our Lord would expect!
>
> We will gather by division for morning prayer. This will be in the hotel room designated by the head of your division, from 6:45 to 7:15, Monday through Saturday. Everyone should begin their workday by coming to morning prayer!
>
> The office will be closed from 5:00 to 7:00 PM. This is mandatory, established as a protection for those who just can't quit!

The afternoon was spent in getting ready —briefing Pete Borel, Carol Showalter, local free-lance writer Harry Lunn,

In the Submarine

and a couple of others who were going to help us; buying a dozen rolls of high-speed film, getting alkaline batteries for the tape recorders, and filling the wagon's gas tank — all things that we correctly surmised there would be no time for, once the conference began. Everything was pretty well under control by five o'clock, when into the lobby of the Muehlebach came Art Lane, Hal Helms, Tom Witter and John Sorensen from home, plus Bill and Carol Showalter and their three children. After a colorful reunion, we grabbed a quick meal at the nearby Denny's and started for the stadium — all eleven of us!

It was seven by the time we finally turned onto 14th Street and headed east. Plenty of time, I thought, until I realized, as we squeezed on to I-70 that thirty thousand other people were doing the same thing. Lord, I prayed silently, I know from experience that the only things that work in heavy traffic are patience and prayer. But I also know that the way the CRS runs things, there will be no ten or fifteen-minute delay; that meeting will start at 7:30 on the dot! And this is one kick-off I don't want to miss, so Lord, I believe, help, Thou, my unbelief! And with that, I did my best to join in the festive air that pervaded the rest of the group. And sure enough, Dean, at the wheel, was able to find an opening here, a quicker lane there.

I switched on the CB. The truckers could not figure out what all the four-wheelers were doing out there, two hours past rush-hour.

"Mercy sakes! We be makin' five mile an hour in this heah parkin' lot! What's goin' on, anyhow? Are the Royals playing?"

"Negatory! Them's be Christians! An' they's goin' out tuh Arrowhead, tuh kick heck outa Satan!"

6

"Write Down this Word"

It was two minutes to seven-thirty, when we reached the Blue Ridge cut-off. I held up our pink press vehicle pass so that the State Police could see it, and that enabled us to cut sharply to the right, and by-pass the long waiting line into the parking lot. Four minutes later, we were parked at Gate E, and on our way inside. All of us were so excited, we were like a family of young kids, heading for an amusement park or a state fair. It was all we could do to collect ourselves long enough to make plans to rendezvous at the wagon afterwards.

The press room was a hubbub of activity, with late reporters trying to get their credentials, and others asking questions and going over publicity photos. Coke and Seven-up were flowing like water. We slipped through into the press box, picked out four seats together, and surveyed the scene below. The west end of the stadium had been roped off, so that all who came would fill the other two-thirds. To me, they appeared to be nearly full, but people would continue to file in for the next half-hour, before the traffic on I-70 finally subsided to normal.

Some preliminary prayers were in progress, and as I watched the photographers in front of the speakers' platform, I suddenly wanted to be down on the field, at the focal point of where it was happening. John had the same impulse, and so we hurried down. The whole stadium was charged with expectation: you could almost feel it radiating from the concrete walls of the long tunnel that led out to the playing field. At the end of the tunnel, we trotted up the steps and out onto the playing field. I couldn't help grinning and neither could John. No sense pretending we were cool professionals; we were thrilled! Walking out to the center of the field, to join the small body of sound technicians and photographers, my feet seemed hardly to touch the ground. I turned and looked around. There was a vast sea of people everywhere, too far away to make out distinctly, yet close enough to feel their presence.

A buoyant young man in his thirties, dressed in a light blue three-piece suit, stepped up to the microphone. According to the program, this was Dick Mishler of the Word of God community, who would be leading the music at the conference. Like a quarterback trying to call signals, he held his hands up for the stadium to quiet down . . . till there was almost silence. People were still arriving, but they were doing so quietly, respectfully, as if they were coming in late to a church service which had already begun. For a moment, everything was still. There may have been prayers and announcements before this, but one sensed that this was the moment, the beginning.

Up in the press box, in a hushed voice Dean noted the same moment into his tape recorder: "The ushers on the field are standing at the foot of each aisle, facing the aisle, which means their backs are to the speakers' platform. Even in the empty sections, they're not turning around to see what's going on, as they've no doubt been instructed to."

In a stirring voice, Dick Mishler called out, "Let's sing together, number two in the back of your programs, 'All Hail the Power of Jesus' Name.' " As the opening strains of that great hymn began, I realized that though I may have sung it a hundred times or more, I'd never noticed how powerful were the words — *All Hail the Power of Jesus' Name* — indeed, every line in the hymn was like a shout of victory! It seemed like I was singing it for the first time, almost as a prayer of exultation! And it felt and sounded like many, many others were experiencing the same thing. There was a lift and a jubilance to it like I'd never heard before — as if Jesus Himself were there, and we could see Him, bigger than life, with His arms stretched out to us, much as the huge banner at the end of the stadium depicted. "Let every kindred, every tribe, on this terrestrial ball, to Him all majesty ascribe, and crown Him Lord of all! To Him all majesty ascribe, and crown Him Lord of all!"

Joy burst upon the stadium, as days, weeks and months of hope and anticipation were released. Any secret doubts I had harbored, that the conference might turn out to be marred by whipped-up, self-generated enthusiasm were banished forever in that opening hymn. And in the press box, Dean had a similar reaction: "I've walked into a lot of football stadiums, filled to the top for big games, but to realize that in this stadium were thirty-five or forty thousand people† who have all come because they love Jesus and God . . . I find it a very moving, overwhelming experience to see all these people —" and his voice broke.

Down on the field, John and I had forgotten the cameras around our necks and were totally immersed in that glorious moment — "We'll join the everlasting song, And crown Him Lord of all." A spontaneous cheer went up when it was over, as if the home team had just scored a touchdown.

The next song was new to me, but was obviously an old favorite of at least the Charismatic Catholics in the audience, which comprised not quite half of the 37,500 full-time adult registrants. It was a fast-tempo, rousing song which lent itself to the guitar — "Sing to the Lord a New

†The attendance was later put at forty-five thousand.

Song." More than just a foot-tapper, it was a dancing tune which brought people to their feet and would become a conference favorite. Dean was watching from the press box: "Well, it's difficult to sit here, and hear and see them singing this song and not want to get to your feet with them . . . I'm watching a priest on the platform, a gray-haired gentleman with horn-rimmed glasses, and he's jumping up and down and clapping his hands and dancing . . . obviously very, very happy in his God — and mine."

You wouldn't think that it would be possible to dance in a stadium, what with the rows so close together. But people were finding ways, and one of the ways was to cooperate, to dance together, in a sense. And so whole long rows were swaying to the left and to the right, in time with the music. It was an astonishing sight to behold, looking up from the field, to see entire rows moving as one. Some would be moving to the left and others to the right, but all would be moving in time with the music, so that the overall effect was harmonious. It looked like the surface of a rippling stream, and it was indescribably beautiful.

Another surprise and delight was the black oval scoreboard, suspended above the west end of the stadium. It was computerized, so that it could display stationary messages or moving ones and present line drawings in black on white, or reversed. It could even do a passable job of reproducing likenesses from photographs, which meant that those in the furthermost seats could know what a featured speaker looked like. This sign, which could have been a dreadful, garish intrusion, instead proved to be just the opposite, amplifying and deferring to the speakers' platform, and reflecting the spirit of what was being said or sung. The messages were flanked by illuminated ads for gasoline and cigarettes, and while at first this was an irritation, most of us soon came to see the Lord's sense of humor in it, for were we not called to be in the world but not of it? And as the board would frequently proclaim, truly Jesus was Lord!

After "Sing to the Lord," Dick Mishler, sensitive to the moving of the Spirit, and aware of the power of music to focus the mood of a large assembly, called for two quieter songs, loved by Charismatics of all denominations — "Thou art Worthy," and "He is Lord." Again, we put all our hearts into them, and you could raise your hands and just feel the presence of God! Dean, in the meantime, had left the press box and gone down on the second level to be among the people in the stands. "The crowd is standing and raising their hands to the Lord in a quiet, worshipful song, this time," he recorded. "I see tears in the eyes of many, as they sing humbly and reverently," and from his voice, there were obviously tears in Dean's own eyes as well.

As the last strains died away, a beautiful, clear tone began high in the uppermost tier at the east end of the stadium. It swept lightly down through the stands and out onto the field, where it was picked up by Dick and the others on the platform and all the rest of the stadium. In lilting, soaring harmonics, the tone lifted and subsided, like a cascading fountain of pure, clear, living water — forty-five thousand people were opening their hearts and singing in the Spirit.

Joining my voice to the others, my scalp tightened at the thought that never before in history had so many hearts together poured out their love for Jesus so freely at the same time! I gazed up at the stands, turning slowly from extreme left to extreme right, trying to assimilate forever the incredible sight of so many people glorifying God. In the highest rows, I could barely make out the raised arms of worshippers, silhouetted against the darkening eastern sky.

We were in "the heavenlies" — an expression I never particularly cared for, but there was no better way to describe it. And I had the feeling that we were being accompanied. I'd had such a feeling before, singing Handel's *Messiah*, and some of the other great Church music, in our choir back home, and sometimes singing in the Spirit. But

"Write Down this Word"

this evening, looking straight up into the blue-black sky, it was somehow easier to imagine angels joining in — and not just a few, but a whole host, extending upwards, tier upon tier . . .

It came to an end, as it had to, but I felt like we were still up there, with the stadium far below, an elliptical bowl with its green field barely visible in the gathering night . . . The Lord Himself brought us back down to earth, with a word of prophecy, given in free verse through someone in the Word Gifts Group:

> Mark down this day and remember it,
> And write down this word and recall it,
> Because my promises will never fail,
> And no word that I speak falls to the ground,
> But I will fulfill it, every word.
> Remember it, call it to mind, declare it publicly;
> Have no fear, because I am faithful to my word,
> And I will fulfill it.

> I am going to restore my people and reunite them.
> I am going to restore to my people
>   the glory that is mine.
> So that the world will not mock it or scorn it,
> But so that the world might know
>   that I am God and King,
> And that I have come to redeem and to save this earth.

> Yes, mark it down and remember
> That I have told you that I am restoring my people,
> Bestowing upon them power and glory,
> Bringing back to them the glory
>   that is proper to my people,
> And making them look again like a kingdom,
> The Kingdom of God on this earth.

The schedule of preliminary speakers that evening was arranged to briefly yet dramatically put the Charismatic Renewal in historic perspective and also give witness to its breadth and depth in all denominations. Two grand old Pentecostal preachers, Howard Courtney, who was a member of the planning committee, and Bishop Samuel L. Green of the Church of God in Christ, acted as co-leaders of the evening's agenda. The opening speaker was Vinson Synan.

"I'd just like to mention that we have three great streams here together tonight . . . They began on the very first day of the Twentieth Century, not far from here, in Topeka, Kansas, in a Bible School called Stone's Folly, conducted by Charles Fox Parham." He told of the class's discovery that in most cases in the New Testament, when the Holy Spirit came, He brought gifts with Him, notably the gift of speaking in tongues. A young girl asked Mr. Parham to pray for her, and that was the beginning of the first stream — the Classical Pentecostals.

He next summarized the Neo-Pentecostal stream, which had surfaced in the late Fifties and early Sixties, and of the Catholic Pentecostal stream which had begun just ten years ago, he said, "Of all the things that God has done in this century, I think this is the most surprising to me!" And the stadium was filled with laughter. "Now we have these three streams here tonight together, and what a miracle we are seeing before our very eyes!"

Pauline Parham spoke next. It was her father-in-law who was leading the prayer meeting in Topeka, when the Spirit fell upon them. "It was just seventy-seven years ago, a few miles out of Kansas City, when a group of Holiness people gathered together, seeking God with their whole lives, that they might have another Pentecost . . . My father-in-law and mother-in-law spoke many times of the great light that filled the room. In those days, they used coal-oil lamps, but this light was brighter than the noonday sun. And as many as were filled with the Holy Ghost, tongues of fire sat over their heads as they worshipped God. They sang in many languages, in harmony, and in the power of the Spirit, and God was glorified."

Pauline Parham was followed to the microphone by Patti Gallagher Mansfield, who was at the Duquesne retreat, when the Spirit first fell among the Catholics. On Saturday night, they were having a birthday party, but she had felt drawn upstairs to the chapel. "As I knelt down, I became aware of the majesty and holiness of God in a way that I had never experienced before . . . I uttered a prayer of surrender. 'Father, I give my life to you. I surrender my life to you. Whatever your will is, that's what I want to do. I want to follow your Son, Jesus, whatever it means, and if it means suffering, I accept that, too. Just teach me to love as you love.' The next moment, I found myself prostrate before the altar of God, flooded with the strength of His tremendous personal love for me . . . Within an hour, the Lord sovereignly drew all the students from the party downstairs to the party upstairs."

In between these small but brilliant crystals, which were strung like jewels on a necklace, there were brief prayers, sometimes praise, and sometimes music, so that one never had a sense of speaker being piled upon speaker. I rejoined Dean in the press box, but when he tried to tell me some of his impressions, he was stopped by the depth of his own emotions. Carol shushed us and pointed to the speakers' platform. On the north end, the fifty or so musicians were ending a song, and from the opposite end, where the planning committee sat behind the Word Gifts Group, came Brick Bradford. He told of a landmark conclusion reached by a study committee of the United Presbyterian Church some seven years before: "We are convinced that the work of the Holy Spirit is not only a vaster topic than can be addressed by one committee of the Church, but points to a neglected area of thinking and practice. It is very possible that the Holy Spirit is preparing a renewal of the Church in our time that may come in surprising ways and through unexpected channels."

That unintentionally prophetic word had come as a real encouragement to a little band called the Presbyterian Charismatic Communion, which had formed four years before. Committed to bringing additional spiritual renewal to the Presbyterian denomination throughout the world, today their members were to be found in practically every Presbyterian body. "We fully realize that the Lord has called us to be one," he summed up, "just as He and the Father are one. And we honestly pray that we shall not be guilty of further fragmenting the Body of Christ. Therefore, we are endeavoring to contain some of the present-day Pentecost in existing structures, knowing very well that the Lord is quite capable of removing or changing those structures at His appointed time and in His own sovereign ways." In response to which, there was much applause.

I rubbed my chin. I was going to have to give expression to a tiny, dark cloud that had been nagging at the back of my mind. No bigger than a man's hand, it was growing, and I sought to allay it, before it robbed any of the sustained joy I was experiencing. "Hey," I said to Dean, "have you seen them pass out any of the order forms for our book?"

"No, come to think of it, I haven't."

"Well, when are they going to?"

"Probably around the time they take the collection," he shrugged.

"What do you suppose happened?" To my knowledge, this was the first instance of even a minor wrinkle in CRS planning.

"I don't know — maybe there were too many people coming in all at once. That was quite a crowd —"

"And for that matter, when are they going to announce

the book? I mean, isn't the time for announcements over?"
Dean frowned and smiled at the same time, which signalled that he was thoroughly exasperated at my questions. "How do I know? Look, we're missing what's going on."

I turned back to the field, but at the back of my mind the cloud was growing larger. Bishop Green was introducing Mike Evans of the Messianic Jews. He was a young, exhortative speaker, and he received great applause for his opening statement: "There are more Jews than we have ever fellowshipped with or known before, worshipping the Messiah, praising the Messiah, and praying in the Spirit, because of *your* faith, and because of *your* love."

He then shared a vision that he had recently received. A Jewish man was standing alone in the middle of the desert. He was alone, in great agony and pain, and demon forces were consuming him. There was a great body of people interceding for him, but they were behind a large pane of glass. "All of a sudden, I heard a great blast of the *shofar*, the ram's horn, and this group just broke through that glass! That Jewish man turned in three directions. And when he turned, the demonic forces lifted, and he started running out of the desert . . . His flesh was whole, his hands were lifted in praise, and he was smiling and crying. I knew he had found the Messiah, and the Spirit of the Lord was upon him.

"He turned and looked back towards the desert, and two glorious swords came into his hands. He turned and walked back into the desert, but this time the swords were whirling. The further he went into the desert, the faster they turned, till he had reached the place where he had been before . . . Demonic forces again came to consume him, but they couldn't touch him, because the Spirit of the Lord was upon him. And as this battle raged, the ground started cracking, and tens of thousands of Jewish people started coming up from the ground, crying and weeping and naming the name of the Messiah, and rejoicing in God!"

There was much applause and some shouts of "Hallelujah!" for this vision, and members of the Word Gifts Group were impressed to read resonant passages in Isaiah and Ezekiel. They then took a collection, solemnly informing the assembly that as of that moment, the conference faced a deficit of a quarter of a million dollars. I peered down through the glass of the press box; no order forms were being handed out, as far as I could see. The dark cloud now covered my whole horizon.

Dennis Bennett would be the next speaker, and I decided to go down on the field. As I passed through the press room, a weary Ronn Kerr said, "Well, we got over three hundred. In fact, we've run out of rooms for them. But they're being really great about it, doubling up. A Los Angeles *Times* fellow just left to find the Omaha *Herald* guy, who's going to share a room with him, that sort of thing."

I congratulated him and hurried for the down elevator, which was just closing. Out on the field, there was more singing in the Spirit, and as it soared, suddenly they added extra floodlights to the bank of lights that was already illuminating the field. But the new light seemed to magnify with the singing. I am not saying that there was more light there than was being produced by the floodlights themselves, but I'm not saying there wasn't, either.

Dennis Bennett stepped to the microphone. He spoke of the historical — and inescapable — traditions of the Church "Sometimes a dear Christian friend will say, 'I'm just a New Testament Christian,' and then they'll begin to talk like Calvin and Luther and Thomas Aquinas and Cranmer. And you know, you hear all the history behind them coming through, because they've been formed by twenty centuries of Christian tradition, and there's no way to get around it."

Afterwards, Jamie Buckingham, speaking very slowly

and with great tenderness, led a prayer: "Let's just stand together and remain quiet for a moment. I'm going to ask you to reach out and touch the person closest to you — take a hand, or lay a hand upon a shoulder, as a sign of our unity. As He touched us, so we touch one another. And as the oil on the head of Aaron ran down his beard to the hem of his garment, as the dew of the Mount of Hermon descends to the Mount of Zion, so with our unity we bless Thee, O God. Amen." There was a moment of silence, then grateful applause.

A little after ten, Howard Courtney introduced the keynote speaker of the conference, Kevin Ranaghan, who would deliver the main address. Speaking forcefully and dynamically, Kevin covered much of the ground that he had outlined to Dean and me at lunch, but there was another communication going on, on a level far below the words that he was speaking. And although those words were strong and right, they could not adequately express what was being communicated on the heart level.

"The Lord called this assembly so that each church would receive a witness to what the Holy Spirit is doing within it . . . We are a people — and we want the churches to hear this — who long for, hope for, work for, and are willing to die for our churches, so that the universal Church of Jesus Christ can be renewed and built up . . . He had decided to have *one* people, *one* bride!"

There was tremendous applause, as he got to the heart of the matter — and the conference. "Now this unity is not something which we have accomplished. The unity that we have here tonight is a gift of God; it is a great work of God in our day . . . It is something that we need to guard with our humility and our repentance and our openness to one another . . .

"I do not mean to say that we are still not, in many ways, a divided people. We *are* divided. There are many elements of faith and practice and culture on which we are not yet one. But I believe we can be one, that the Church can be one. It's not an impossible dream; it's the will of God that we be one!

"We've got to realize that this unity is happening here tonight. We know that the Holy Spirit is making us one, and many powerful streams are, in fact, flowing together. All these streams we've been talking about — we have to realize that by the power of the Holy Spirit, God has dug some canals between those streams! God has opened the floodgates to allow huge bodies of water to flow into one another. And tonight, the people of the Spirit are coming together, flowing together. The work of the Spirit is meeting up with the work of the Spirit, and the power of the Spirit is meeting up with the power of the Spirit. And now, tonight, it is all coming together, like a mighty river, thundering over this Arrowhead stadium waterfall. And it will flow forward from this conference. It will flow out of here a mighty river, and it will burst across the face of the nation and, indeed, the world, as we go forth from here a *newly united people!*"

Cheers and tumultuous applause greeted this declaration, and he closed with this prayer: "O Lord Jesus Christ, you *are* our Lord! How glad we are to proclaim it tonight! O Lord Jesus Christ, be *more* our Lord. Help us to turn over more and more of our lives to your daily Lordship and guidance. Help us, Lord, to be more obedient, and for you to be our Lord means that we *must* be obedient . . . O Lord Jesus, you love us, and we love you, and we want to obey your commandments. O Lord, teach us in this conference to truly love one another, so that the world may know that we are truly your disciples. And so that, seeing us one in love, the world may believe that you, Jesus of Nazareth, are Savior and Lord. Amen."

The people were tired; it was close to eleven, and many had been there for five hours and more. But as one, they rose to their feet in a standing ovation. And the rest of the conference would take its lead from that speech.

That night, going back to town, our wagon may have been loaded to the brim, but our spirits were soaring. Art Lane, the Episcopal priest from our home community, confessed that he had never really felt comfortable, raising his hands in praise of God before. He had done it, but more out of obedience than anything else. But tonight he had raised them — chest high at first, then shoulder high, then all the way up. And he had experienced a freedom that he had never known before. And Hal, a Congregational minister, and Tom, a Presbyterian minister, were both bubbling over about the sincerity and spontaneity of the joy they had seen all about them. As for John, he had run through all of his film and most of mine, capturing the night on film, and Dean could hardly even speak of the evening without choking up.

Only their driver was less than completely free in the exhuberance of the moment. For, to my knowledge, they had never passed out the order forms, though the book announcement did come at the very end, along with instructions on where to board the conference buses, as people were concentrating on filing out of the stadium.

The dark cloud that covered the horizon was rapidly approaching.

7

A Corporate Gift

It was nearly midnight, when we finally pulled up in front of the Muehlebach, but no one felt like going to bed. We may have been dog-tired physically, but our spiritual batteries had received such a charge that we could have gone for three more hours before running down — and more than a few did.

Jamie Buckingham happened to arrive at the hotel the same time I did, so I asked him for his impressions of the evening. "I thought the show of unity was very impressive," he said, after thinking about it for a moment. "I came into the meeting with a fear that someone would use it as a platform to spread their own particular brand of Christianity. When none of that occurred, I came away with a good feeling about the meeting. I thought what Dennis had to say from his own traditional background was very good." He paused, and I became somewhat belatedly aware that he was very tired and was having to make a conscious effort to marshal his observations for me. Chagrined, I determined to curtail it as quickly as possible.

"Kevin's speech was really fine, *very* good," Jamie emphasized, "but for me what was bigger than all the speeches, what overshadowed the whole thing, was the people. To be in the middle of that place with that mass of people around, and to know that everybody was involved . . . you know, I've been in so many churches, even Charismatic churches, where only the folks in the front rows sing. You get half a dozen rows back, and the singing stops. But to be on that platform tonight, and to see all the way to the far back, and to the highest seats in the uppermost balcony, people with their hands raised against the sky — I just stood there and had to bite back the tears.''

I thanked Jamie then, and he went straight to bed, as he would be leading one of the nondenominational meetings in the morning. But I was still wide awake and went looking for Dean. I found him with the Showalters, at a place which would become our late-night rendezvous in nights to come — standing in line outside a tiny ice cream parlor called Topsy's on 12th Street.

Dean turned in before too long, but it was after one, before I abruptly ran out of gas. In the elevator on the way up, I knew I would regret having stayed up so late, because I had told Dean that I would take a shipment of Rock Harbor books to the UPS office first thing in the morning, and they opened at eight o'clock. And two hours after that, I was due to pick up Dennis and Rita Bennett and take them to the airport, while Dean checked into the order forms. That was quite a coincidence, I thought; I had happened to be standing by the speakers' platform at the end of the program, when Dennis came down. Knowing that he was leaving in the morning, I got a nudge to offer him a ride, with the thought of getting an uninterrupted interview. He had been delighted, and relieved to have that item taken care of. Well, Lord, maybe you're in charge, after all, I thought.

As I got into my bed that night, I stared at the dark ceiling, fully awake. You know how certain songs that hit you when your emotional receptors are wide open, seem to play over and over again? Sometimes you'd be glad to be rid of them, but other times, like tonight, you didn't mind a bit. "Sing to the Lord" was one of them, and accompanying it were images I hoped I would never forget — of 45,000 people singing and dancing their complete joy together in Jesus Christ. It was, in fact, a wonderful way to fall asleep.

Six hours later, rosy-fingered dawn reached in, parted our curtains, and splashed sunlight all over my pillow. Wearily I got up and slipped silently into my clothes. The cartons of books to be shipped were in the back of the wagon, so I got it out of the underground garage across the street and headed for the 12th Street viaduct. And as I did so, I did something very foolish. I can't remember what I was thinking about at the time — probably resenting the fact that I didn't get to sleep in, too — but as I turned right onto the viaduct and raised the turn signal indicator with my left hand, for some reason I held it up there as the steering wheel returned to normal. This broke the mechanism that shut off the turn signal, when the turn was over; in fact, it broke the turn signal completely, as subsequent testing revealed.

"Blast!" I slammed the steering wheel with the heel of my hand. To be without a turn signal in downtown Kansas City, or shifting from lane to lane out to Arrowhead with eight or nine other people in the car, wasn't just an inconvenience; it was downright dangerous. Of course, one could drive with the window open, using hand signals, but with no air-conditioning, that was going to be one miserable trip . . . I wondered if there would be a dealer who would have a turn-signal mechanism in stock, how long would it take to get it fixed, how much would it cost, and how Dean and I would ever be able to take care of it with everything else that was going on.

A Corporate Gift

In the end, I gave it up to the Lord — after all, what else was there to do? I told Him I was sorry for having such a negative, resentful spirit that morning, and I even asked Him to fix the turn-signal indicator, reminding Him that I was about His business when it happened. But I checked it again on my next turn, and of course, it still wasn't working. I did my best to put it out of my mind, until I could do something about it. I got to the UPS office just as it opened, and found that the cartons I needed to ship were one pound under their hundred-pound limit to the same address. That was a surprise worth praising God for, so I did, a little, and the thought came to me to ask the girl behind the desk if she knew of a car-wash. It was a ridiculous question, because we were way down in a desolate area, several miles from anywhere, but because the wagon was filthy, and I had an hour and a half before I was due to pick up Dennis and Rita, I asked anyway.

"Funny you should ask that," the girl replied, "because right across the street are two men who will give you the best car wash in town. They're off the beaten track," she said, smiling at the understatement, "but we send our vehicles over there all the time."

I thanked her, and thanked the Holy Spirit, too; He seemed determined to help me, in spite of my surliness. Well, okay, I thought, smiling. I left the wagon, and walked half a mile to a truck stop, to get a cup of coffee and a look at the morning paper. *Joyous Union of Faiths Rewards Long Journeys* read the banner headline across the front page, with a four-column, very appealing photo of three young people praying. The byline was Helen Gray's, the religion editor who had done a nifty job of presenting the overall picture through a variety of capsule reactions, like that of a nun from the Fiji Islands, Sr. Rufina Medina, who explained that she had come to learn "how to give the Baptism in the Holy Spirit to our people. I'm also expecting to have a clearer idea of how to deal with the healing ministry." The overall effect of story and photographs could not have been better, and it was obvious that the paper had decided to take an extremely positive point of view, regarding the conference.

I picked up the wagon, sparkling clean, and arrived at the designated entrance of the Muehlebach at precisely ten o'clock. There was Dean, standing out in front with Dennis and Rita, and another Episcopal priest. This turned out to be Bishop Bill Frey, whose diocese was in Colorado, and who was going out on the same flight and also needed a ride. I knew that of all the Episcopal bishops, Bishop Frey was known to be the most sympathetic towards the Renewal, but I was surprised to learn in the course of our trip that he himself was the head of several "extended households" which were living "in community". Moreover, the people in his diocese were sufficiently relaxed about it to gently kid him about it in a skit performed in some annual diocesan affair.

Once we were packed and away, I asked Dennis how he felt about how the conference was shaping up. Like Jamie, he had come "with some trepidation, because I really didn't know what the nature of the conference was going to be. I didn't know whether it was going to be truly interdenominational, or whether it was going to be gently dominated by one group or another. And I was very pleased to see that although the Roman brethren are certainly beautifully coordinating things, they're really *not* dominating, and neither are any other groups. On the contrary, it seemed to me to be a genuine mixture, a good, healthy representation of all the various power structures in the Renewal. So, I would say that this is certainly the finest large conference that I have ever attended."

How would he put the conference into the overall, historic context of the Renewal? "We have a fruition here of many years of growth in the Renewal. And incidentally, it's *not* a movement. We've been called the Charismatic Movement, which we aren't. There is no movement, no central structure, no bosses, no growth fund, all of which was another thing that pleased me about last night: there was no focusing on any one man as *the* man, nor does there appear to be in the rest of the program."

"In honor preferring one another," commented Bishop Frey, and I told him that that was the verse we intended to use in the book's dedication, as it exemplified the planning and preparation of the conference. I mentioned that the People of Praise had been working on the conference for more than a year, and that there seemed to be a corporate call upon their community, to serve the Body of Christ in this way.

"They've had that kind of experience with big conferences," Dennis agreed, "more than any of us. I think that what they did was, they *gave* to the rest of us, what they had developed."

A corporate gift . . . What did Dennis see coming as a result of the conference? "Of course, the test of any conference like this one is what happens when people go home. And my continuing concern is that people realize the Charismatic Renewal is something happening *in* the churches. It is not a new church, it is not a new denomination, it is not a new anything. But last night reassured me that the Renewal *is* healthy in the churches and is working where the Lord wants it."

Bishop Frey, who had said very little up to that point, spoke then: "I saw the Renewal beginning to come of age last night. It got out of the adolescent stage and started to have some real maturity in it. Which is only measured by this humility that you've been talking about. And that's the true maturity."

Since they had a little time, they invited me to wait with them at their departure gate, so I parked the car and joined them. When it came time for them to leave, Rita asked me if I would pray for them. Feeling wholly inadequate, I silently asked the Holy Spirit to give me the right words.

We all joined hands, right in the Kansas City airport, and I prayed that the Lord would send travel angels to protect them, that He would rest and refresh them, and powerfully anoint them for the ministry he had called them to. And then Bishop Frey prayed a blessing over me — the first time a bishop had done that since my confirmation, some twenty-seven years before. I turned away before they could see how moved I was.

Driving back to town, I noticed that the turn-signal indicator was working.

At twelve noon, Dean and I had an appointment with Fr. Bob Hawn, the executive secretary of the Episcopal Charismatic Fellowship. At ten minutes to twelve, on the far side of Truman Road, I finally found a parking place. At two minutes to twelve, I was entering the Music Hall, out of breath and soaked, and there was Dean, waiting for me. He took me back to the wings, where we waited until Bob's meeting was concluded.

He took us to one of the dressing rooms, and I asked him if he had been able to get much sleep last night. "No, about three hours. People wanted us to talk, and then other people wanted to share, and so it was after three before we finally got to bed. And then we woke up at six," he sighed and smiled. "But the Lord takes care of it all."

Was he pleased that nearly three thousand Episcopalians had registered? "Yes! Especially when you stop and think that in terms of the economic situation now, it's really getting to be a problem for people just to make these conferences. Because, even though we try to keep the fees down, it's still an awful lot for transportation, for housing, for food. I just praise God that people will make the sacrifice to come."

What was different about this conference? "Well, aside

from the fact that it is the first time in history that so many denominations have come together in this way, I think it is probably the first time that any differing Christian bodies have ever come together without some sense of reservation, or defense, or hostility. I feel this is a true miracle that God has worked into this conference, and He began to work it in the planning committee. When a few of us began talking about this three years ago, it seemed to us that if we were *truly* open to the Spirit, we could do such a conference without crossing over and stepping on people's toes in the denominational, doctrinal areas . . . because if we're led and guided by the Holy Spirit, *the Spirit does not lead into division or into disruption.*"

Dean and I both commented on the truth of that, which we had not seen quite like that before. Was there anything in particular, which struck him about last night? "Well, by now you're familiar with the operation of the Word Gifts Group. But you might be interested to know that up until three hours before the meeting last night, there was no Word Gifts Group assembled! Each of us on the planning commitee individually submitted names of people from our denomations whom the Lord was maturing, whom He had worked through, and who would be open to what He might want to do. The group was finally assembled only two hours before the meeting."

"That close?"

"And these people were from all different denominations!" Bob added, growing even more enthusiastic.
"Many of them had never seen each other before, and now they were gathered in a room by themselves, to pray and praise the Lord. The power that I felt in that room before the meeting was stronger than anything I'd previously felt in such a room. And Kevin, when he addressed them, said that he had never felt such power. Usually in a large conference, it's the second or third night before that group really begins to open up, and the Lord

begins to work through them. Last night, the moment they got on the platform, the Lord started doing things, and we did not have enough time to begin to present all the things that were coming through them!"

It was too bad, I thought, that they hadn't built some unallotted time into the agenda. What did he see coming out of the conference? "I see the Lord calling us to come together as His body, to witness and serve the world. And this coming together to praise the Lord in unity here is going to be the stepping-stone for the same thing to happen in each city that we go back to. Now let's get on with it!"

We thanked Bob for putting it so clearly and directly, and let him get to where he was supposed to be for lunch. As we left, it occurred to me that Bob and Dennis and everyone playing a part, were contributing to the corporate gift.

Back in the office that afternoon, we ascertained that a number of the order forms had indeed been passed out by the ushers as people were leaving, possibly as many as thirty thousand. What had happened to the rest? Someone thought that Joe Heintzelman had seen that the remainder had been distributed around to the sites of the ten denominational conferences that morning. But someone else said no, they thought that they were still in their cartons, out at Arrowhead, and Joe himself was not available to ask. We began to look at the possibility that we might have to print another ten or fifteen thousand forms to hand out at the denominational conferences, which was now the only feasible way to get them into the hands of interested persons. We called Larry House, but he was out, showing some out-of-town visitors around the conference, and they had no idea when he would return.

In the meantime, we talked to Rocky Scofield, a local volunteer, who was in charge of food service. At the noon meal, two hours before, all the months of preparation had received their first test — how had it gone? Rocky beamed. "In less than an hour, they had passed out eight thousand lunches in the Municipal Auditorium/Bartle Hall area, and ten thousand others were distributed elsewhere. All morning long, there has been the most incredible grace on all the workers I'm responsible for. In fact, I was just talking to Joe on the phone, and he said what a blessing it was for him, that all the food service workers were right where they were supposed to be." No wonder he was beaming!

"There's been a spirit of praise around here all morning," he went on. "You'd be here for a while, and pretty soon, over in the workers' lounge, you could hear people just starting to worship God. And it was the same over at the workers' headquarters at Grace and Holy Trinity Cathedral; every three minutes or so, they'd just stop and pray."

We had to leave then, as we wanted to check out the workshop Fr. John Bertolucci and Sr. Ann Shields were leading in the basement of the Holiday Inn. When we got there, the room which was supposed to hold 225, appeared to have nearly double that number; people were standing against all the walls, and there were forty or fifty out in the hall, hoping to catch a few words through the open doors.
The size of the overflow was even more impressive, because it was sweltering down there. The air-conditioning was totally inadequate, and it must have been well over 90 degrees. Yet instead of going to a less crowded workshop, they stayed right there, hanging on every word, as Fr. John described the unique way in which the Holy Spirit brought the Renewal to his little Italian parish in upstate New York.
I was able to hear only the very end, but what I heard explained the rapt attention. Big, stocky, and possessing a keen sense of humor, Fr. John was telling the story of St. Rocco:

"I had arrived on the parish scene only a month or so, when these beautiful Italian ladies came up to me and said, 'You know, Father, we have a custom here. Every year, we celebrate *La Festa di San Rocco*.' Now somewhere in my childhood I remembered the statue with the dog and the bread and the wounds, but I don't know if he's real, or if he went the way of Christopher and Philomena . . . So I say, like all those involved in the Charismatic Renewal who find themselves in a quandary, 'May I pray about it?' "

Fr. John was on the horns of a dilemma. As much as he would like to accommodate his new parishioners, Rocco was *not* on the liturgical calendar, and he did not relish the prospect of bringing that old, colored statue from the back of the church into the modern sanctuary. He was especially reluctant to do so, at a time when what he really wanted to do was find a way to emphasize the centrality of Jesus and lead them into the fullness of the Renewal.

Two weeks went by, and the ladies again came to him and said, "Father, we noticed that you were upset. And we've decided that you don't have to move the statue. Leave it where it is, but let's have a nice celebration."

So Fr. John went back to his study, to find out about St. Rocco. He took down the "Official Book" — the *New Catholic Encyclopedia*, and to his astonishment, he discovered that Rocco was real. And not only was he real, but he had been converted at a mission and had given his life to the Lord Jesus Christ, and was filled with the Holy Spirit. What was more, he had discovered a whole new life of prayer, and had suddenly, very mysteriously, begun praying with people — as a layman; he never became a priest or brother, never even took vows. But he began to lay on hands as he prayed, and people started getting healed. And one of those miraculously healed was the Pope's brother! With that, Fr. John clapped the book shut, exclaiming, "Oh, Lord! Are we going to have a celebration!"

As the night of St. Rocco approached, Fr. John went into Utica, which has a large Italian population, and got *canoli* and *espresso* and all the makings of a first-class feast. He planned his liturgy with equal care: first lesson, Peter and John, praying for healing, in Acts 3; second, lesson, Jesus commissioning His disciples to go forth and heal; homily, a talk about the healing power of Christ, and how it was transferred to the disciples and apostles of the early New Testament Church, and on down through the centuries, to an eighteen-year-old boy named Rocco . . . .

In the meantime, the Lord brought back to Fr. John's church an eighteen-year-old boy whose life had been transformed by the Renewal — a living witness to the healing power of the living Christ.

The night arrived. Word had gotten around that something special was going to happen, and the church was packed out. And so, Fr. John told them about their beloved St. Roc, in a way that they had never heard before, and the young man gave his testimony. And when they'd finished, Fr. John said, "Because this is the feast of St. Roc, this young man and I are going to lay hands upon anybody who wants to come down that aisle and pray for healing — *just the way Rocco did.*"

Every single man, woman, and child came down the aisle, and for two hours Fr. John and his young friend prayed and laid on hands. And that was how the Renewal came to a little church in upstate New York.

When he finished the story, there was joyous applause and even cheering, and I thought to myself that although the Empire Theatre, where he and Sr. Ann would be tomorrow, held four times as many, when the word got around, it wouldn't be big enough. (And it wasn't.)

It was nearly an hour before the crowd around them finally thinned out. They were praying for and fellowshipping with a little paraplegic boy named Joey, on whose face was a radiant smile, and when they had finished, Dean and I brought them glasses of ice water. We asked if they could possibly spare a few minutes more, and when they agreed, we found a quiet place. Neither of them was a stranger to large conferences — what did they think about last night?

"I was in tears at some points," Fr. John said, and Sr. Ann, who was a coordinator of the Community of God's Love in Steubenville, Ohio, and a member for twenty years of the Religious Sisters of Mercy, nodded her head in agreement. "I wept, too," she said quietly.

"And did you notice how easy it was to bring the people to praise last night?" Fr. John asked. "Easier than at any conference I've ever attended, including our own." He paused to take a drink of water. "For me, that stage down there was the symbol of the whole conference. Because on that stage was every possible variety of brother and sister in Christ that you can imagine. It was a mini-Kansas City Conference right there. And these brothers and sisters were publicly saying, 'We love one another. We're working together on this platform in a way the world has never seen.' And that's true . . . that stage was a symbolic pointing toward the fulfillment of the prayer of Jesus: that all might be one."

We turned then to Sr. Ann, who had been doing some thinking. "I was at the conference in Rome two years ago, when there were prophecies given that were to become a substantial directional force for the Catholic Charismatic Renewal. They spoke of a coming darkness, though they were not prophecies of doom and gloom, but rather to prepare us for a time of darkness that would also be a time of victory," and she, too, took a sip of water. "Anyway, they have had a maturing effect on us, in having us look at our lives and our communities and a lot of things, seeing what is shakable and what is unshakable, in the sense of Hebrews 12:27, where it says that only the unshakable things of the Kingdom shall remain. And apparently, the same sort of maturing has been going on in the other denominations, too, because what I've been experiencing in Kansas City is more and more people saying, 'God, what is your word? How do you want to lead us into unity? Whatever it costs, I'm going to follow you.'"

We remarked that we also had sensed an attitude of "We've talked about it enough; let's start *living* it."

Sr. Ann concurred. "It was the same in our general session this morning. A sense of God saying to us, 'Don't hear my word, as though it were good advice, and you can pick and choose what you want to accept and what you want to let be for a while. When you hear my word, you are to embrace my whole word.' You've got to take everything that it calls you to do, and know that He'll give you the power to do it. It's *not* the kind of word where you can just say, 'Well, that's an excellent opinion.'"

"It's not optional any more," Fr. John stated. "As Kevin said last night, this conference itself is a prophetic word. We are seeing the prophecy. A man on the bus said to me today, 'I'm going to be disappointed if we don't get some clear direction from this.' What he's saying is that he wants some spoken prophecy that's going to give it to him, A-B-C. He completely missed what he was *seeing*. What we're talking about is sacrament, which means sign, and the conference is a sacrament, in a sense of what is going on in the whole Body of Christ. For instance, I've discovered that I can be Catholic *and* ecumenical, and I used to think there was conflict in that. But here we are not into the differences; we admit that they're there, but we're on another level, the level of love. You know Jesus. I know Jesus. You are my brother! We'll work our problems out, hand in hand. And we *will* work them out, because it's no longer optional. We are obliged to do so. Because the command is to love one another."

It was five-thirty, and we needed to get what was left of our order forms to some key locations, before we went out to Arrowhead. We thanked Fr. John and Sr. Ann, and Dean carried a batch of forms to the bookstore, while I took some to the Muehlebach. When he came back, he told me that he had run into John Boughton, who had just finished tallying the number of orders for our book in all three stores at the end of the first full day.

"How many?" I asked, afraid to hear the answer.

Dean shook his head. "Eight hundred," he said.

The dark cloud which had been looming ever more ominous, now totally engulfed me. I tried to remind myself of all the big and little miracles which had marked the project every step of the way. I tried to confess my unbelief and give it up to God. I tried to accept His forgiveness for it, and pleaded with Him to change my heart, and even praised Him for the eight hundred copies. But it was no use. All I could think of was that there were only two more days left, plus a couple of hours on Sunday. Two more similar days (*if* enthusiasm did not wane) would yield only twenty-four hundred orders altogether — less than half the number we needed to break even. Our embryonic publishing company now faced the certainty of bankruptcy, before it even had a chance to show what it could do. Stillborn, was the word that came to mind.

Dean was concerned also, but far less than I. As usual, he responded with swift, practical action, calling Larry House to tell him that it was now definite: we had to have fifteen thousand more forms by tomorrow morning. The only trouble was, Larry was still out, so all we could do was leave the message. We also tried to call Dan De Celles, to ask them to please plug the book again, but it was too late: the office was closed. "Well," Dean said, "we're just going to have to trust the Lord."

But that was one thing I was no longer able to do.

Cardinal Suenens

Arthur Katz

Larry Christenson

Bruce Yocum

Ruth Stapleton, Pete Borel, and Francois Celier

with George Cornell of the Associated Press

Members of the Aqua Viva Community
of San Jose, Costa Rica

Kevin Ranaghan

Bob Mumford

Jim Forbes

Francis MacNutt

8

"Repent and be Healed"

We were going to try to get out to Arrowhead a little earlier, this second evening of the conference, because Dean and I had received permission to be with the Word Gifts Group, as they prayed and sought the Lord for an hour before the meeting began. Trying was the correct word, because not everyone was ready, and our number in the station wagon had been increased by two more ministers, who were friends of our home community — Ron Minor, pastor of the Cambridge Presbyterian Church, and Dave Emmons, who ran the United Church of Christ's retreat house at Bristol, Connecticut.

I was annoyed that we were late and annoyed that, counting the Showalter children, there would now be thirteen in the station wagon, and annoyed that we didn't seem to be getting enough interviews and could not possibly cover everything. But as I sat there while we waited for a couple of stragglers, tapping the steering wheel with my finger-tips, I knew perfectly well that those petty annoyances weren't the real problem. They were merely surface chop, beneath which loomed the dark form of the leviathan that had been trailing our little ship ever since it had left Rock Harbor, two weeks before: failure. I had always had an irrational fear of large things under the sea, ever since a shark had bumped me, when I was playing in the surf as a young boy. Now I was about to be consumed by one.

"David, I don't know what it is, but it really seems like you've been striving lately — rushing here and there, trying to control everything, very much in your self. You've not been flowing in the Spirit at all — what's the matter?" It was Carol Showalter speaking. And as with others close to our community, we had an unwritten covenant that we would care enough for one another to speak truth, as the Holy Spirit led. I had spoken strong truth often enough to Carol, and now she was speaking some to me. The trouble was, it was the last thing I wanted to hear just then, and it was all I could do to keep from exploding at her.

Yet even as my anger mounted, I knew in my heart that she had spoken out of Christian love; I would have done the same in her place, and had, many times. And what made me maddest of all was that her discernment was right on.

Should I tell her? Open the can of worms in front of everyone? I was tempted. Get the whole thing into the light, so that they could help me be free of it, and I might again experience the sweet joy that was on the faces around me. The relief would be worth whatever it cost in pride, my heart seemed to be telling me. But too often darkness prefers darkness, and instead I chose to hide behind a screen of plausible explanations and put on a happy face. And for a while I did feel a little better.

As it turned out, we reached Arrowhead in plenty of time, and Dean and I went down to the game-film reviewing room on the field level, where the men and women of the Word Gifts Group were assembling. They were led by Bruce Yocum, one of the coordinators of the Word of God community, who complimented them on how well things had gone the night before and had one word of advice: "If you feel impressed to share a reading from Scripture, don't

"Repent and be Healed"

feel that you have to share the entire chapter." There was gentle laughter. "Just the key verses will do."

And then they got down to prayer. It was silent at first, then a tender singing in the Spirit. The sense of God's presence was strong — even I was aware of it, in the state that I was in — and there began to be prophecy calling for brokenness. One man, weeping as he spoke for the Lord, likened the stadium to a basket of eggs, ready to be hatched. But the shells were still intact, not yet broken. They had to be broken, to release the new life within them. A woman, under a quiet anointing, also called — entreated, really — for repentance, that we might be cleansed and come into new joy.

My own heart was struggling to respond, but my unbelief hung round my neck like a millstone, and my head was preoccupied with facts, figures and decimal points . . . Larry House was probably out there in the stadium somewhere, which meant that he wouldn't get home until midnight. Even if he had no other job set up on his press and had all the paper and ink he would need, he wouldn't be able to start printing until morning. Then the ink would need most of the day to dry before he dared perforate the forms . . With luck, we might be able to get them around to the denominational conference sites Saturday morning. Which meant that, even if they did plug the book tonight, there would be no forms available tomorrow . . .

Who did we think we were? A little, back-pocket operation out on Cape Cod, with no offices, no staff, nothing but two guys with the dream of starting a Christian publishing company . . . I mean, what were we doing here?

Someone else was speaking a word of prophecy at that moment, and in an agony of despair, I did something I had done only once before, while someone was prophesying: in my heart I cried out for a word from God.

The very next words out of the speaker's mouth were:

"Do not disparage small beginnings!" And the prophecy returned to its somewhat milder vein.

I was stunned. God had answered me — with the stern rebuke that I so roundly deserved, so that I knew beyond a shadow of a doubt that it was Him.

For a moment, I felt as if my heart had stopped beating. The Lord had jolted me out of the pit of despair. All my fibrillation was stilled now, waiting for the steady beat of faith to return to my heart. But nothing happened. It was time for the Word Gifts Group to go out on the field, so half in a daze I followed Dean upstairs to watch the opening proceedings from the press box. Carol had saved us a couple of seats, but no sooner were we comfortably ensconced than I got a nudge to go down onto the field. Which I did.

It was very strange, the way I felt. I had a peace of sorts, at long last, only it wasn't that peace which comes with trusting God or resting in the center of His will. It was more like a selective numbness, which had deadened all sensitivity in the area of concern about the book project and left me perfectly alert everywhere else. It was as if God had given me a shot of spiritual novocaine, to enable me to get on with what He had called me to do.

I noted that it was cooler this night, and there didn't seem to be quite as many people as the night before, though it was still an enormous crowd. Once again, the singing brought everyone to their feet, and it felt like we were picking up exactly where we left off, the night before. And now, there was a strong word of prophecy:

"I speak a word of repentance to my Church. I am not pleased with the state of my Church, the condition of my people. There is much separation, there is suspicion and hostility among you, there is fear and mistrust among you, there is argumentativeness among you. This should not be so, my people. I call on each and every one of you to repent, to turn away from the sin of unforgiveness, of hardness of heart . . .

"If you do not repent, I am going to discipline you. I am going to show you where you stand sinful before me. It is important that you repent; it is important that you turn away from all these sins that keep you separated from your brothers and sisters. Now is the time for you to turn away from these sins. I will give you the understanding, the strength that you need, the healing that you need, to be one people.

"And now I speak a word to you who lead my people. I have the plan, and I have the vision, and I have the way to make my people one. It is not your ideas, it is not your thoughts, it is not your plans. And it is important for you all, you who lead my people, to be on your knees before me, to humble yourself before me and seek my plans, seek my vision for my people. I want you to take counsel together, in all humility, to seek my plan and my vision for my people. I am holding you responsible to seek me on behalf of those I have given you to serve.

"This is a time of repentance for you all, to turn away from all that separates you from one another, to seek me, so that you can be bonded together in true love and brotherhood."

There was a smattering of applause, which Charles Simpson, the evening's master of ceremonies, gently curtailed: "That's a good word to hear, but it's a — hard word to hear. Let's just quietly ponder this word from the Lord." In the ensuing silence, the thought crossed my mind if the Lord had really meant for the leaders to actually get on their knees right there and then, but the program soon resumed. A little later, a second word of prophecy came:

"My people, my people, my people: it is sin that has divided you, and it is the effects of sin that keep you divided. I call you tonight to new life, to new wholeness. I call you tonight to make a decision, to decide to repent, to repent and be open to my healing power. For I have empowered you to wholeness and fullness. This night, my people, repent and be healed in my love."

There was hardly any applause after that, and Charles Simpson, reading the gravity of the moment, said, "We've asked the Lord to speak to us, and I believe the Lord has spoken to us. I also believe it's important that we respond to what the Lord has said. If you believe that, will you say Amen?" And there was a subdued "Amen."

"I believe it would be good if we would just take a moment to invite the Holy Spirit to come and search our hearts and lead us to repentance. Repentance is a gift from God. We can exercise our will by forgiving; we can exercise our will by submitting it to the Lord Jesus, but then the Holy Spirit must come and do a work. I want the Holy Spirit to do that work in me tonight. Do you feel the same way?" And again there was an "Amen," a bit louder this time.

He then led a prayer of general repentance, asking God to search our hearts and help us to confess our sins, especially jealousy and judgment. He asked God for forgiveness, and for help in being open and honest, in seeking out brothers and sisters with whom there had been misunderstandings. And he asked for help in carrying this out, and in learning how to, in honor, prefer one another.

I thought to myself, as he finished, that through that prayer, he had opened the way to corporate, as well as individual repentance, on behalf of the whole conference. But I sensed that the repentance which God had called for, was not ended with that prayer; indeed, it had only begun.

I rejoined Dean and Carol in the press box. With Ruth Stapleton on the program, I wanted to be where I could share impressions with them, and I also knew that every seat up there would soon be taken. Bob Hawn was the next man to the podium. He shared briefly about the birth of the Episcopal Charismatic Fellowship, but it was something he said in his opening remarks that really touched me: "We live in a society which has taught its male members that it is unmanly to cry. But I tell you from my own experience that when Jesus gives the gift of tears, it's a most marvelous and wonderful thing. Last night, I sat here looking at your faces as we began to sing 'Thou art Worthy,' and the tears welled up in my eyes and started to run down my cheeks. My wife turned to me and looked and said, 'I've never seen you cry before!' "

Howard Conatser, the pastor of a large Baptist church in Dallas, followed him, and he, too, spoke of weeping. He referred to a time seven years earlier, when he was on the verge of leaving the ministry, and the Lord had begun to soften the hardness of a lifetime in his heart. "Little did I recognize what God was doing within my heart in the next six weeks, because suddenly the word of God came alive to me, and I walked all over the state of Texas, crying like a baby and wondering what in the world was taking place."

Lord, I thought, as he went on, what are you preparing us for? But it was not to be then, not yet.

"Hey!" Dean said, nudging me with his elbow, "get a load of this!" Striding purposefully to the podium in a flowing white cassock came the most striking figure of the entire conference. You could almost hear the stadium catch its breath. This was Fr. Francis MacNutt, and the first thing he said was: "I couldn't be dressed in black to talk about healing." And then he issued an impassioned call to the clergy of all denominations, not just to talk about healing and pray general prayers for healing, but to have the faith to go out among the people and lay on hands, and let themselves be used by God as channels for His healing.

By way of illustration, he told of an incident that had happened five years before, when he had been part of a team of six who had gone to a place called Blue Cloud Abbey in North Dakota, to speak on Charismatic prayer, which at that time was still a new thing in the Catholic

Church. They were speaking to a group of forty-five priests and a bishop, when three Indians who had been healed in a prayer group just the week before, happened to walk in on their meeting by mistake. They were two women and an older man, and the women testified to what the Lord had done — and healing blind eyes was not the least of the miracles.

Then the older man got up and gave a simple testimony of how God had saved him from alcoholism. He looked around the group of priests without speaking, one by one, and he asked how many of them believed in Jesus Christ? They all raised their hands. Then, for his own information, he asked, "How many you men ever heal anybody?" Two men raised their hands. The old Indian looked at the rest and couldn't believe it. "How come, you believe in Jesus Christ, you no heal nobody?" And that was the challenge Fr. MacNutt offered the churches: *How come, you believe in Jesus Christ, you no heal nobody?*

I almost wondered for a moment, if he would walk down from the platform and over to the long row of wheelchairs that lined the south side of the field. But I realized he couldn't, without completely disrupting the very tightly scheduled program. When he finished, he left the atmosphere of the stadium charged with expectancy.

Ralph Martin spoke next, in what proved to be the briefest address of any of the evening meetings. All he wanted to do was remind us that the Catholic Charismatic Renewal began with the prayers of an ecumenical Protestant prayer group, and that it was Pentecostal ministers and Full Gospel Businessmen who helped bring the Renewal to Notre Dame and Michigan State. That was no accident; God had planned it that way, because He wanted us to know that we needed each other, and that it was *together* that we were going to reach the world for Him.

Some announcements came next, including a good plug for the book, both from the platform and up on the scoreboard. I whispered to Dean, "You know, no matter what happens, we can't say that they didn't really do their best for the book, in promoting it. Here I was afraid they'd forgotten it, and they did a better job than if we'd written it for them ourselves." And my own eyes welled up.

There was more singing, and if possible it seemed even more infectious than the night before. They were singing one of the up-beat, minor-key songs that I assumed came from the Messianic Jews, and as the music increased its tempo, we noted that across the way, whole rows had their arms across each others' shoulders. By doing this, they were actually able to dance to the right and to the left. Looking at the speakers' platform, I laughed aloud; they were dancing around so hard that they would have to be careful or someone was going to dance right off the edge! Even in the press box, there were a number of Christians who could no longer contain themselves and were standing up and joining in, with their arms upraised — to the astonishment of the secular press! Well, that's another first for the Kansas City Chiefs' stadium, I thought; there had already been quite a few.

As Ruth Stapleton came forward to speak, flashbulbs went off all over the stadium, and the assembly rose to its feet in a standing ovation. In front of the platform, television camera crews had joined the swelling ranks of photographers. All at once, I felt sorry for her. Even as she was getting such a big play, I sensed that there were many, many people out there, waiting to see if she merited it. She was wearing a simple, blue knit dress, and she stood erect with a great deal of poise, which made her seem taller than she really was. She started to speak, and whenever she said anything quotable, there would be a surge of typewriters from the top tier behind us. Then they would quiet down again, to listen.

What she was saying was so simple, so direct and so clearly from the heart that an incredible thing happened:

the Holy Spirit reduced that whole vast stadium to the size of a family living room. Listening to her share one commonplace incident after another, not afraid to appear foolish or admit that she was a sinner, you could close your eyes and imagine yourself in a prayer group at a friend's house. And the more she revealed of her own shortcomings, and how Jesus was more than able to cope, in all circumstances, the more we opened our hearts to her.

One story which particularly touched me was when she talked of the time right after the infilling of the Holy Spirit. "For most of us, this is a time when we begin to really praise the Lord. We go to prayer meetings, and we go to Charismatic meetings, and we want to fellowship — sometimes we haven't got quite as much wisdom as we need in those early days, but we have a lot of fun, and we have a lot of joy.

"I know in my own life, after I first experienced that new life and joy overflowing, all I wanted to do was just be with people who were filled with joy. I used to go from one prayer group to another... A good friend, Tommy Tyson, was speaking all over North Carolina, and it didn't matter to me if it was five miles away or two hundred miles away, I had to go, and I had to hear Tommy. And I went, and I went, and I praised the Lord, and I said Hallelujah, until one night I started out of the house, and my poor husband said to me: 'Ruth, come over here and sit down on the sofa just a minute.' "

Ruth went over and sat down next to him, and he said, "Honey, do you have so many needs in your life that you have to go out every single night for prayer?"

"Yes," she said to him, "you just really don't understand."

Her husband put his hand on her head then, and said, "Jesus, whatever is ailing her, would you please heal her now."

We all laughed, and I felt many of us were recalling our

own early exuberance. She then shared some dramatic accounts of healings, and when she finished, there was silence in the stadium, and the tenderness and compassion of Christ was more tangible than at any previous moment in the conference.

It was past ten, and Larry Christenson had still to deliver the main address, but I noted that no one was leaving. I went down on the field, but about ten minutes later, I got this nudge to go back up. I ignored it; after all, I'd just come down. But the agitation wouldn't quit, so finally I went to the elevator. There, waiting for the elevator, was Ruth Stapleton, accompanied by the security man assigned to her.

I was startled at how beautiful she was, and all of a sudden I got tongue-tied — something which hadn't happened to me since dancing school. Desperately, I tried to think of something to say, anything to start a conversation, but nothing would come. The elevator arrived, and we got in. This was ridiculous! Here, the Lord had arranged an exclusive interview — something which we had been informed would not be granted to any of the Press, with no exceptions — and I was speechless. We had only one more floor to go — Lord, help!

"Is that a good tape-recorder?" Ruth broke the silence, pointing to the compact piece of equipment in my hand.

"Yup," I replied, holding it out to her. Good grief, I sounded like a parody of Gary Cooper!

"Because I'm thinking of getting one," she went on, "and I want to get a good one."

"This is a good one," I managed, feeling like I was trapped inside a wooden dummy.

"Yeah," the security man chimed in, "that's the best there is." Now we had a regular conversation going — what more did the Lord have to do?

"How much does it cost?" Ruth asked, as the elevator

came to a halt. I told her and with all my might tried to force some more words out, any words, as the elevator door opened, and they got out. "G'night," I mumbled and smiled sickly, and rode to the fifth floor. I didn't even want to go to the fifth floor!

When I told Dean and Carol what had happened, Carol burst out, "*You?* I don't believe it!" and she scolded me soundly. Dean just shook his head. But then he remembered some good news: Larry House had had him paged in the press box and was starting to print right away. The order forms would have to dry overnight before he dared perforate them, but they would be ready by eleven. Which meant that if everything broke just right ...

Though Larry Christenson's address started off in a light vein, it was a thoughtful message. He began with a poem he had written, about all of us occupying a house for the Lord, rent-free, with different kinds of doors. Some were on the other side of the house, like the one Jesus had recently been knocking on, labeled the Lordship of Christ. "Why has the Spirit brought this emphasis on practical obedience and the Lordship of Christ in the Charismatic Renewal? Because Christians have been dispensing too much of what Dietrich Bonhoeffer called 'cheap grace'. Just believe in Jesus. It's all free. No obligation. No discipleship. No trouble. No demands. No suffering. Smorgasbord Christianity — take what you like and leave what you don't like ... Why does Christ come knocking on doors on the other side of the house? Because He wants to balance what has become one-sided."

A little further on, he quoted Martin Luther: "If I profess with the loudest voice and clearest exposition every portion of the truth of God, except precisely that little point at which the world and the devil are at the moment attacking, I am not confessing Christ, however boldly I may be professing Christ. Where the battle rages, there the loyalty of the soldier is proved; to be steady on all the battlefront besides, is mere flight and disgrace, if he flinches at this point." It was hard to believe those words were written four centuries ago.

Larry returned to military imagery, to make his final point. "Jesus wants a people who have learned to deny self in order to serve the Body, not only at the personal level, but also at the denominational level. He wants a people who have moved beyond personal deliverance to disciplined obedience, beyond blessing to battle-readiness.

"God is readying His people for battle. A group of us were traveling in Israel recently, and passed by one of the many *kibbutzim* that dot that tiny land. We'd all heard about them, of course — small, tightly-knit, highly disciplined and highly dedicated communities that are both thriving centers of life and production, and also form the country's first line of defense. One of the brothers with us made the observation that the history of Israel offers many parallels to the life and history of the Church . . . Throughout Christendom, God is raising up committed, dedicated bodies of believers. It is not a new denomination, and it never will be. It is a network of outposts, strategically placed throughout the land, thriving centers of life but having a level of dedication, selflessness, and discipline so that the Lord can count on them in a special way in the day of battle.

"The form and style of these bodies is varied, as are the *kibbutzim* in Israel. You may find one of these outposts in a non-denominational fellowship, or an Episcopal parish, or an ecumenical community, or a Baptist or Lutheran congregation. They are not linked organizationally, but by a common sense of the Lord's purpose and moving in our day.

"And these outposts do not exist for themselves, but for the sake of the whole people. We learned that Israelis who live in the *kibbutzim* number less than three percent of the population. Yet they have contributed more than fifty percent of the nation's leaders, and more than twenty-five percent of her casualties, in time of war.

"In this, and in many other ways, the Lord is preparing His people for battle. For the tide of evil is rising. The spiritual hosts of wickedness are massing their forces in awesome array. If we did not know that the Lord was also working out His strategy, our hearts would fail us with fear. But He is at work. Quietly, He is going throughout the length and the breadth of this land, knocking, knocking, knocking . . ."

9

The Touch of God

Friday morning — I was back in the conference office, and back in the pit of despair. Dean had gone to get the forms, and I had drafted and received approval for an announcement to be made at the twelve morning conference sites. But it didn't matter, because Dean was not back from the printer yet, and it was already eleven-fifteen. Even if he came right through that door, I thought, there was no way we could get those forms and announcements around to all twelve sites before they broke up at noon. Nor would there be any percentage in trying to disseminate them to the twenty-eight workshops this afternoon. The best we could do was shoot for tomorrow morning; at least that way, we'd get one full day.

But you know how sometimes, when your intellect explains to you that further effort is pointless and you ought to just quit, your heart refuses to face reality and keeps on hoping on its own? Well, my heart was like that; it just kept praying its own prayer, ignoring my head and believing that somehow, even at this last moment, God would work it out. And my will, which was sitting in the middle like a tennis judge, knew that when my heart got that way, there was no reasoning with it. And so, it went along with my heart, and

I kept hustling — lining up the assistance of three messengers and the use of an extra vehicle, and praying like mad that God would somehow bring Dean to the office immediately. It was eleven-twenty.

Just as I was ready to throw in the towel, Dean came in. He had tried to double-park, couldn't, and to save time had pulled into the indoor garage next door, only to be unable to find a place to park for thirteen floors. Then he had to get the fifteen thousand forms back up the slowest elevator in Kansas City.

Moving and talking as fast as we could, we briefed the messengers to take the forms and announcements to the facility managers at the Little Theatre, the Music Hall, the Municipal Auditorium, and the Muehlebach. Dean would head out to the trade mart and cover the three sites there, dropping me off at Bartle Hall on the way. But that still left Kemper and the Pentecostals out at the Governor's Exposition Building. And then, out of nowhere appeared Dick Key, an associate of Bob Mumford's, who asked if he might be of any assistance.

"Can you take some forms out to Kemper and the Exposition building?"

"Sure, no problem." And by eleven-twenty-five, we were out the door. Ten minutes later, Dean dropped me off at Bartle Hall, and I headed up the escalator. I was stunned at the size of the crowd. It was rated for 10,500, but there must have been considerably more than that; there were people as far as the eye could see. And there was a beautiful spirit in the hall, a very strong yet tender presence of the Holy Spirit that seemed almost visible, like a silvery haze.

For an instant, I was awestruck — what was happening? But I didn't have time for that. My luck was holding: in that huge place, I was able to find the facility manager right away. I explained my problem, gave him the approved announcement, left a carton of forms for him, and asked directions to the Lutheran conference. They were next door, and again my luck held; I was able to deposit forms and announcement in no time. The Methodists, downstairs, took a little longer, but incredibly, the job was done by ten minutes to twelve.

I went back upstairs, to see what was going on at the Catholic meeting. I still couldn't believe we'd actually gotten all those forms and announcements around in time — and then I noticed the carton of forms right where I'd left them. The facility manager had been unable to get the announcement up on the speakers' platform.

I pleaded with him to try again, and looked on as he was again being turned away. It was exactly noon — too late. I turned away myself then, and went over and sat against the wall. All hope was gone now, and I felt completely wrung out and used up. I didn't blame God; I blamed myself for not having heard Him at all, for having called myself to this project, instead of being called —

"Before you leave," the public address system said, "we have an announcement: order forms for the special book about the conference, *Like a Mighty River*, will be available by the down escalator . . ."

Did I hear what I just heard? My eyes filling as the reality of it sank in, I could not find words to ask God to forgive me. I just sat there, shaking my head, overwhelmed by His love. Gradually I realized that the whole room seemed to be filled with a heavenly benediction. The others present had been experiencing it for some time, and I was finally on their wave length.

There was a spirit of healing in that vast hall, and now I was beginning to see what I was looking at — everywhere, there were people in clusters, praying, their arms around one another. There were priests praying for laymen, laymen weeping together, circles of people around needy individuals . . . The Lord was walking through that place, pausing here and there, touching this one and that one, healing. (It was only much later, listening to a tape of that morning meeting, that I learned what had happened: Fr. MacNutt had responded to his own challenge, and the Holy Spirit had, in effect, turned the meeting into a communal healing service.) And in passing, the Lord had paused by my side, forgiven my unbelief, and touched my heart.

For the next half-hour or so, I wandered around among the crowd with a lopsided smile on my face, lost in the wonder of God's love. I ran into fourteen men and women from Costa Rica, who informed me in halting English that they were from the Aqua Viva Community in San Jose, the first Charismatic community on Costa Rica. I snapped their picture for the book, and Jose Miguel Arias did his best to explain how they happened to come: "The Lord, He want us to come here." Had He made it possible? "Yes, we saw His hand in everything. In prophecy, He told us, 'I will give you the money, bill over bill over bill.' " And had He done so? "Yes," he replied simply, with quiet reverence.

Later, I talked to Bill Winegard, of the Lamb of God community in Baltimore. Bill had been involved with the Renewal for some time, so it was especially significant, when he said, "I have never seen such a presence of the Holy Spirit; it was the most moving session of my whole life. I myself am not given to overt crying, but I had my handkerchief out, along with all the rest . . . . I think one of the most moving things I saw was a man in a wheelchair struggle out of his chair and over to a friend in another wheelchair, to grasp him, while the two of them prayed. I've just never seen anything like it!" he said, shaking his head. "And that sort of thing was going on throughout the entire room. It wasn't that you had a healer up on the platform, 'healing' everybody; *people were healing each other!*"

(Indeed, I was later to hear of a number of reports of miraculous healings. But since I was unable to check them out personally, I've decided not to report them secondhand. The healing I experienced in my own heart, however, convinces me that there must have been hundreds, perhaps thousands, of healings of mind, body and spirit.)

A little late, I remembered that I was supposed to meet Dean for lunch, and so I hurried over to the Muehlebach, where he informed me that we hadn't eaten since noon the day before. We grabbed a hamburger and agreed that he would cover the press conferences with Cardinal Suenens and Ruth Stapleton, while I roamed the workshops.

The first thing that happened was, I ran into Dick Mishler, of the Word of God community, who was responsible for leading the singing at Arrowhead. I learned that he was a last-minute substitute for Jim Cavnar, whose wife was having a baby. And Jim Berlucci, who would normally take over the song-leading in Jim Cavnar's absence, was unable to do so, because *his* wife, too, was having a baby. I observed that it was God who decided when babies came, so perhaps the Lord had worked it out that way.

"It might be," Dick admitted. "I grew up as a Protestant, and learned a lot of those basic hymns, like 'All Hail the Power of Jesus' Name.' Yet when I came to know the Lord in a personal way, it was in a tiny Pentecostal church, out in California, and I learned the old favorite choruses, traveling around a lot, speaking and holding revivals in Assembly of God churches. And then as a Catholic, which I've been for twenty years, I've gotten immersed in the kind of music that's coming up through the Renewal. So looking back on it, God seems to have prepared me for this particular assignment."

I commented on how I had gained a new appreciation for the way music influenced a meeting. One song could change the entire direction and flow of the mood. How did he know what to call for and when? "I seek the Lord about what He wants to have next, and sense how His Spirit is moving . . . Yet I try to prepare in advance, too. If one of the Messianic Jewish people is going to share, we do one of their songs. And I have notes on the length and mood of each song — worshipful, rousing, gentle, or even explosive; sometimes you come to a point where you just cut loose with one. But mostly, it amounts to coming to what the Holy Spirit is giving us guidance on at the time."

After leaving Dick, I poked my head into the back of Peter Marshall's workshop. Most of the two thousand seats were taken, and he had just gotten to the intermission of his talk on "Growing up into Christ." I spoke briefly with one of the women coming out of the meeting, Laura Woodger, of the Redeemer Lutheran Church in Buffalo. What did she think of what she had just heard? "Well, it is something that is providing me with an awful lot of food for growing up . . . I really thank God that He is inspiring him so much, to be able to share so much of himself with all of us here." How did she happen to come to the conference? "Well, I found out about it last year, when I was at the Lutheran Conference in Minneapolis . . . and the Lord opened up the pathways for me to get here."

From there, I went over to the main bookstore, beneath the Municipal Auditorium. Even though the workshops were all back in session, the place was teeming. There must have been nearly a thousand people, browsing among the endless book tables. I ran into Rod Williams there, the president of the Melodyland School of Theology. "I just hope that the churches would understand that what has been happening here is not a threat to their existence, but that these are people of God, who have no desire to stand outside, or fight in opposition to what's going on. They are a kind of leavening influence on the Church . . . . I really hope that the churches can sense this denominationally, that this is a stream of reality and vitality flowing into the

The Touch of God

life of the churches, and how can you fear that?"

The room for Bill and Carol Showalter's workshop on Christian marriage held only six hundred, but it was packed out. They were telling how husbands and wives needed to be totally open and honest with one another, to hear the truth as well as speak it, to be prepared to be the wrong one. They confided to me later that they had an excellent example to start off with: fifteen minutes before their workshop began, they were arguing so vehemently about what they should start teaching on, that as they rode up the escalator to the room their workshop was in, they took their name tags off so that no one would know who they were! And when they shared that with their workshop, the place broke up with laughter. Apparently, more than a few had had similar experiences. The trick was, Bill and Carol said, to get one's feelings out in the open, where Christ can deal with them, not to stuff them down.

My last stop that afternoon was the workshop of Bill Beattie and Judy Tydings on an introduction to the Catholic Charismatic Renewal and the Baptism in the Holy Spirit. Both Bill and Judy were coordinators of communities, Bill of the Alleluia community in Georgia, and Judy of the Mother of God community in Maryland. The workshop was pretty well over by the time I arrived, but I listened to them field some tough questions with considerable poise and good humor.

They needed both poise and good humor, it turned out, for an incident which they related to me, as we walked back to the Muehlebach. Their workshop had been in the old Empire Theatre, and Judy was speaking, as a fat rat wandered sleepily out on stage from the wings behind her. She didn't see it, but some of the audience did, and Bill, noting their response and its cause, moved slowly, so as not to disturb Judy, and with a gentle, well-aimed kick, lofted the rat back into the wings. We all chuckled as he related the incident, and Judy admitted that she wondered what on earth he had been doing.

I said goodbye then, and caught a ride out to Arrowhead, to join Dean at the press conference, which was being held in the game-film room. Ruth Stapleton had already been answering questions for nearly an hour when I arrived, and every seat was taken. I stood against the back wall and listened, as the reporters would give their name and the publication they represented, and then ask their question.

The man from *Bible for Today* asked her to comment on the nature and extent of her influence on her brother's spiritual life. "Well, my influence on Jimmy has been exaggerated an awful lot. I have to admit that; I sure would like to take the credit for his born-again experience and his spiritual growth. But Jim's always been a very religious person, a very disciplined person in his religious life, a student of many of the great theologians, and my only influence was that walk we had in the woods, when I shared with him what I felt total commitment was, and the experience of the Baptism."

A woman from the *Catholic Charismatic*, whose name also happened to be Stapleton, introduced herself —

"Are we related?" Ruth asked, smiling.

"That's what everyone's been asking me," her questioner replied, to much laughter, and then she asked if Ruth felt that the Lord was doing a new thing at this conference, and if so what? "I feel that this new thing that Jesus is doing is a deep ministry, a deep work of healing down on the heart level . . .".

George Cornell, Associated Press, wondered what effect her brother's new job had upon his religious life. "I've been with him quite a bit," Ruth answered, "and I don't see any difference before and after. I never dreamed he'd continue teaching Sunday School when he became President, but he's doing it. I really don't see one bit of difference; it's just public now, instead of private."

Pete Borel, Rock Harbor Press, spoke up then (at the instigation of Dean, who was standing next to him): "Mrs.

Stapleton, we have a young man from Paris here who has recently had a three-hour visit with the sister of the President of France. She is a Christian, very much alone, and has asked for counsel. Would you be willing to write her a letter of encouragement? She is very close to her brother and —"

"I'll be happy to," she replied.

Later, Pete had an opportunity to introduce Francois Celier to Ruth. They spoke for no longer than five minutes, but it was the fruition of an extraordinary move of the Lord. Francois Celier was a young French evangelist, in America to observe the conference and staying with Pete, who was acting as his interpreter. Shortly before he left France, he had met with the sister of Valery Giscard d'Estaing, who told him that, short of a miracle, France was going Communist in next March's national elections. She specifically asked him to make contact with those high up in American government, to ask them unofficially for counsel, encouragement, and above all, spiritual support.

Through Pete, Francois said that the situation was similar to the one France faced in 1940, only now she was appealing to America for spiritual, rather than military, aid. There was a tremendous spiritual battle going on in France, and Francois had been given the mission of galvanizing American prayer support for France. But there had been no way that he, as a private citizen, could reach anyone close to the President — until a remarkable series of coincidences, beginning with Rock Harbor Press inviting him to represent them at Cardinal Suenens' press conference, for the benefit of his European point of view. That he had stayed on afterwards, for Ruth Stapleton's conference, was mere coincidence.

(Two days after this, Francois was interviewed on national Christian television, and he told this story, asking all Americans to please pray for his country. And today I note in the latest issue of *Time*, that the coalition between the Communists and Socialists in France, which had seemed so invincible last July, is now being torn asunder by internal strife and bickering. Apparently, the Socialists and Communists are now so antagonistic towards one another, that they would rather lose the election to the Centrists, than share a coalition government.)

While Dean and I waited for the press to vacate the game-film room and the Word Gifts Group to arrive, he filled me in on Cardinal Suenens' conference, which he had taped. The Cardinal had turned out to be a warm and responsive individual, who spoke at the same time with great gravity and maturity. He was introduced as one of the four moderators of the Second Vatican Council, and the man personally assigned by the Pope to act as unofficial shepherd of the Charismatic Renewal in the Catholic Church.

A priest representing the *North Carolina Catholic* asked the Cardinal if he found himself being cast as a protagonist of the Charismatic Renewal, by bishops in America and around the world, and particularly by the College of Cardinals. "Well, in fact, I think I have been the first Cardinal to support the Charismatic Renewal. I had a conversation with the Holy Father some years ago, when the Renewal first began, and he said to me, 'Well, I am waiting for the bishops to make a pronouncement on it.' To which I replied, 'Yes, Holy Father, but the bishops are waiting for you to say something.' So everybody has been waiting for each other, and somebody had to walk on the waters, and that was a bit of my role there."

A little later, Larry Hammond of *Acts 29 Plus* asked what the general feeling of the College of Cardinals was, regarding the Renewal. "Well, I must say, I haven't the slightest idea," the Cardinal answered honestly. "Because the College of Cardinals is very new today. We are a hundred and twenty cardinals, of whom I know perhaps twenty-five, because so many now are from Africa, from

Asia, from Latin America. But the ones I know most, I would say generally favor it . . . I think they will take the same position as the Pope, saying 'It's a chance!' And a chance means something which is not automatically going to succeed. But if you're going to start, if you earned it, if you accept guidance and so on, I think it's a *big* chance!"

In what areas, someone asked, did the Cardinal see the Charismatic Renewal making an important difference? He touched on the Baptism in the Holy Spirit, the renewed love of the Sacraments, new hope for reconciliation, a new healing ministry. And then he said, "Another aspect where the Charismatic Renewal is doing something very important and has already made history, I think is in a renewed image of Christian communities. If I think of a community like the one in Ann Arbor, just to mention one . . . where you see 1800 people, having made a commitment to the Lord and to each other, sharing impartially their goods and so on . . . well, there's something to hope for for the future; it can bring such renewal! In the past we thought that religious communities were something for celibates alone."

By six-fifteen, the reporters had filtered out of the game-film room, and the Word Gifts Group had pretty well gathered, munching on sandwiches and potato chips out of their box suppers, which were actually in bags. Dean struck up a conversation with one of them, a man named Virgil Vogt, from Evanston, Illinois. He learned that Virgil was one of the leaders of Reba Place Fellowship, and of the conference, he had this to say: "Somehow just being here, with all these other Christians makes the reality of Christ and the Kingdom of God — all the things we believe and preach and practice — you know, stronger. It's been a personal encouragement to me, in terms of expanding and strengthening my faith."

At that, the Word Gifts Group began to come to worship. There was singing in the Spirit and some anointed Scripture, and silent prayer. And then there was prophecy, and once again, the Lord was calling for repentance. Another word came, and another, and a man stood up and said that he felt the Lord would convict the assembly to the point of tears tonight, and another confirmed this, saying that he felt the Lord would give the gift of tears. I felt my own heart responding strongly to this, but then someone said, "And He wants us to have worship, and He wants us to have praise —" and the next thing I knew, the focus had eased away from repentance and onto more pleasant things.

10

"Humble Yourselves Beneath My Hand."

As the Word Gifts Group and the planning committee filed out to the speakers' platform, Friday evening, up in the press box Dean recorded the moment on his tape recorder: "Kevin Ranaghan is in the lead, followed by the Cardinal [Suenens] and Bishop Patterson, the black Pentecostal, who, I understand, is the Presiding Bishop of the Church of God in Christ. It seems to be kind of overcast, this late afternoon, but still hot and still clear, so a lot of people must have been praying the rain away. The stadium is already more than half full; there'll be a large crowd tonight. And they're already singing — "Hallelujah, Jesus is Lord!" — with the same enthusiasm and anticipation as last night; in fact, it's as if there hasn't been a day in between. The scoreboard says, 'We have found a wedding ring in last night's offering. If you would like it back, come to the information table behind the orange banner . . .''

Fr. Everett Fullam was the master of ceremonies tonight, and he introduced Thomas Zimmerman, General Superintendent of the Assemblies of God, who led the opening prayer. He was followed by a brief testimony from Nelson Litwiller of the planning committee, who for forty-two years had served as a Mennonite missionary in South

America, before "being told it was time to retire" and coming home to the States. Then the Lord chose to baptize him in the Holy Spirit, "retread his retirement, and get him back out on the road again" — to Nelson's obvious delight. That road took him back to South America twice last year, carrying word of the Renewal, and supported now, not by a missionary board, but by the Holy Spirit moving on the hearts of prayer groups, including Catholics, for whom he had once had very little use.

Nelson was followed by Maria von Trapp, who had some strong words to say about "this terrible Women's Lib movement which is emptying our homes." And then came a word of prophecy — a brief, gentle, imploring word:

"Harden not to the broodings of the Holy Spirit which is in this place tonight, but yield yourselves to that which the Spirit of the Lord would declare and show unto His people. And surely if you would not harden your hearts but yea, yield . . . you shall stand in a new place of insight into His counsels and His ways . . ."

Then one of the Word Gifts Group shared a vision of Jesus marching into the stadium with angels around and behind Him, and His heart was glad with the assembly's praise. Another song followed, and then a second word of prophecy, as tender and beseeching as the first. It, too, spoke of and to the heart:

"It is written in my word that the kindness of God shall lead my people to repentance. And I would dare you into my heart this night . . . that you may know my kindness, and willingly and freely shed the garments of your old ways. I would impart unto you a freshness and a newness in my heart, that my heart and your heart might beat as one. For the mission to which I call you requires that your heart be yielded wholly unto me, that your heart be separated from those things round about, and that your heart express truly what has long been on your lips: 'Thy will be done on earth, as it is in heaven.'

"Come and draw near unto me, that you may know the kindness of my heart, and that you may be my instrument to reveal kindness unto those that yet sit in darkness. Come with willing and free hearts, and shed the garments of your old ways."

As the word of prophecy ended, there was some scattered applause, but most people remained silent, thinking about what they had just heard. It was hard to imagine how the message could have been more loving — *would* we let His kindness lead us to repentance? And then, as if to underscore His call, "Thy Loving Kindness" was the song we sang next — many of us singing that old favorite with new awareness of what the words were saying.

There was yet a third word of prophecy: "I am the great surgeon that works on the hearts of men. Skillfully I will open your hearts, that I may put my seed into them, the seed that will bring forth life in you all. I will cut skillfully yet tenderly, for I love you and care for you, my children. Do not, therefore, resist the cutting, for the seed will bring forth new life, will bring forth new light in your lives. Therefore, my children, do not harden your hearts, but open them to my word that will come to you."

Harden not — there was the same phrase that had opened the first word of prophecy. And all three words were so gentle, so loving . . . the Lord was pleading with us . . .

"Hallelujah!" cried someone on the speakers' platform, "We open our hearts to you, Lord!"

The next speaker was a black man who approached the microphone with great bearing: "My name is Ithiel Clemmons, I am a member of the planning committee, and I am standing tonight to introduce the man whom we feel to be the greatest holiness preacher in the world." He was referring to Bishop Patterson, who began his address by saying, "Thank you, Brother Clemmons, and I am sure the Lord will forgive you for that introduction," which brought great laughter.

Holiness was the theme for the evening, and Bishop Patterson had a few things to say on the subject: "If we lose our holiness, we have lost favor with God, as salt having lost its savor, good for nothing but to be cast out and trod under the feet of men. I emphasize and hyphenate the word Pente-cost, because it is costly." And he reminded us that the founding fathers of the Pentecostal Church knew what it meant to have rotten eggs thrown at them, be shot at, jailed, tarred and feathered — and miraculously delivered from white-hooded lynch mobs. "But they believed that the same God who delivered the Hebrew children from the fiery furnace, and Daniel from the lions' den, would deliver them. Let us hold fast to our integrity. Let us earnestly beseech the Lord that we not only will be gathered here in one place, but that we would be in one accord...."

Next, they made an announcement about the book, and Dean leaned over and told me that as of that evening, they had received 2400 orders. The Old Boy tried to get me going again, reminding me that there was only one day left. But I would have none of it, and instead, thanked the Lord for giving us twice as many orders today as the day before. I thanked Him, too, for the gift of faith. And I sensed, though perhaps it was just me, a new softness and openness in the hearts of those assembled. I was glad that the next speaker was Cardinal Suenens.

Speaking with a Gallic accent, the Cardinal began with a prayer so simple, yet so heartfelt, that he might have been alone, kneeling by his bed. "O Lord, you are the most real person here tonight. You love each of those persons here with all your love. You love your Church in a very special way. You love the unity of your Church. Tonight, O Lord, we are living something precious!

"We are gathered together in your name, the name of Jesus, a name nobody can pronounce without the power and the grace of the Holy Spirit. It is with the power of the Spirit, with all the admiration we can put in it through the grace of God, that I pronounce your name — Jesus . . . Jesus . . . You are the reason of my life . . . I have the joy to serve you . . . ." If anyone had ever wondered whether a prince of the Roman Church could truly be as close to the Savior as a common pauper, that doubt was forever put to rest; indeed, there may have been more than a few of us who envied his closeness.

"The trouble today," he told us, "is not that we are Christians; the trouble is that we are not Christians enough. We have to be Christianized again, in depth, and on that day they will see something of the Lord shining through us. I remember a preacher asking, 'If there was a risk of your being put in prison because someone accused you of being a Christian, would they find enough evidence to support such an accusation?'

"Let us go back together . . . to where the Church started. Let us go back to Jerusalem . . . Jesus, help us just to be faithful to you. Be you my life," he prayed softly, "be you my eyes, be you my ears, be you my mouth, be you my heart, be you my breath, be you my hands, my arms, my feet — Jesus, help me to go and to speak your word, in your holy name, in the power of the Spirit. Christians, speak! Speak powerful in the power of the Spirit! The world is dying, because it doesn't know the name of its Savior, Jesus Christ! Amen!"

There was stunned silence, then cheers and hallelujahs rent the air. Dick Mishler called for one of the Hallelujah songs, and the scoreboard joined in on the chorus. Down on the field, people along the sidelines formed a chain and danced to the music. In between pieces, I interviewed the youngest worker I had yet encountered, a sparkling-eyed lass of thirteen, very grown up, with a spray of freckles across the bridge of her nose, named Valerie, who was the daughter of Tony Rowland. What did she think of the conference? "I love it! Just being with all kinds of people is a lot of fun and excitement."

What was the most exciting thing that had happened so far? "Being able to work on the field." I noticed that her identification badge said *Assistant to the Arrowhead Manager*, and that she carried an imposing walkie-talkie. Did she talk on that? "I take the calls that come through," she informed me solemnly.

"I see," I nodded, suitably impressed. "Have you had any problems with it?"

"No, I haven't had a call yet."

"Oh," I bit my lip, to keep a straight face. "Um, what's the hardest part of your job?"

"Running around with him," and she indicated Fr. Ed Sylvia, the person responsible for the Arrowhead facility, who was standing nearby. "It's a big job," she assured me, "because he runs around a lot himself, and I have to run after him."

"I see," I said gravely, "so you're kind of his runner, you might say."

"Right," she nodded pertly, indicating that the interview was terminated. I thanked her, shut off my recorder, and went up to the press box. It was already ten, and Bob Mumford was due to start the final address at any moment.

As I rode up in the elevator alone, I wondered about the spirit of repentance that the Lord had seemed so desirous of visiting upon us, earlier in the evening. Those three prophecies right in a row, and then the grand move of the Spirit, during Cardinal Suenens' speech — we had veered close several times, but did not seem any nearer than before.

Outside the press room, in the hall, I stopped for a moment to talk to Gloria Murphy and Kay Frey, the girls responsible for the speakers and special guests, and they both commented on how the pace was finally beginning to take its toll. They realized that they had been running on sheer nervous energy since Wednesday, and talking to them, it dawned on me that Dean and I had been running on one meal a day for the past three days ourselves. So I went and got a container of popcorn.

"Here, have some dinner," I said, putting it down in front of Dean, when I rejoined him in the press box. He yawned widely and thanked me, and we settled down to listen to Bob Mumford. He, too, was concentrating on holiness, which he defined as *dedicated involvement.* "It's when I get involved with what God is doing with my whole person, body, soul, mind, and spirit," and he went on to sketch some of the things that hindered holiness. At the top of the list was secular humanism — "it's more of a threat than Antichrist, Communism, or anything else you could ever describe. Secular humanism has man at its center . . . it's when *the world evangelizes the Church.*"

The second hindrance was individualism — living in our own little private worlds. The third was loss of vision, the fourth was lack of unity, and Bob saw these as progressive phases in a man's journey away from holiness.

Next, he listed the helps to holiness. First, there was God's Word as our life source; second, the change from "me" to "us"; and thirdly, "I want you to see a victorious Lord . . . In the early days of Pentecost, we had a siege mentality, content to get inside our four walls, nail the door shut, and wait for Jesus to come. The Lord said, 'No, I want you to take a sneak look at the back of the book,' " and Bob pantomimed opening a book to the last pages and gasping at what he discovered there. "Hey!" he shouted to the furthermost rows, "How many of you know that if you take a sneak look at the back of the book, *Jesus wins*?" And the stadium rang with cheering, as if Jesus had just won the Super Bowl!

Instead of waiting for them to subside, Bob shouted, "Amen! Hallelujah! Glory to God!" and entered wholeheartedly into their enthusiasm. "Glory to God, glory to God!" he cried over and over, laughing and praying in the Spirit, and the crowd responded. "Do you believe that?" he shouted, and the affirmatives came rolling back on a wave of whistling, arm-waving and applause. "Jesus is Lord, Jesus is Lord, Jesus is Lord!" Bob chanted, clapping his hands in rhythm, as he repeated the theme of the conference. And the crowd picked it up.

They were shouting and clapping their hands over their heads now, and I went down on the field, to be closer to the center of it all. When I got there, it was still going strong, but now the crowd began to sing a new song on their own, and Bob had to rein them in. "No, no, no, hey, hold it, hold it, hey, church, please? Hold it, don't do that now." and they finally began to heed him. "Come on, just sit down, please, right there." And they did. "You just had a Holy Ghost breakdown, that's all," he explained with a chuckle, and the crowd roared with laughter and settled back into their seats.

"Now, the next thing," said Bob, returning to the heart of his message, "is *the sacrifice of unity* . . . there are some things we *can* sacrifice in order to have unity, and there are some things we don't feel we can sacrifice, is that right?" And the crowd signalled their affirmation with applause. "There are doctrinal differences, there's policy and habits, and ways and manners of worship, and various forms of liturgy, etc. But see, that's not what our problem is.

"Our problem is, we have not been willing to sacrifice for unity in the realms where we really and truly can . . . The Body of Christ depends on all parts coming together in a functioning, working relationship. We are not talking about one world church. We are not talking about absorption. We are talking about fellowship and coming together in the unity of the Spirit. Amen?" And the crowd cried Amen and applauded.

"I'm asking, in Jesus' name, if you want to know the life of holiness, you're going to have to learn something of what it means to love one another." And he wound up his address by teaching on the Scriptures which emphasized this point. When he finished, there was another boisterous demonstration for Jesus and a couple of songs, and then a word of prophecy from the Lord that seemed to cut directly across the mood of the crowd:

"The Lord says, if you are to follow me, then you must hear the word that I speak to you now. You need brokenness, my people. Yes, you need to be broken, to move forward with me in the way that I have chosen. As a mule is stubborn, refusing to go along the path that his owner desires, so there are resistances among you, my people, to the way that I have chosen.

"I see pride among you, my people. In some of you, I see pride for what you've attained and what you've accomplished in following me. I see haughtiness, and I see defensiveness that will not allow you to move into the unity that I desire for my people. I tell you, *this must change!* I see a willful spirit among you, that prefers its own plans to my own, a spirit that prefers the comfort and security of what I have already done among you, and will not move forward into the things that I desire, unity and love within my body. And I tell you, my people, this cannot be. These things must change among you. Your pride needs to be broken. Your will needs to become pliable in my hands, that I might form and shape you according to my purpose, and not your own.

"Yes, listen to me, my people, and move forward in the way that I show to you now. Humble yourselves beneath my hand and desire a spirit of meekness and a spirit of humility, a spirit that is teachable, so that I might move you in the direction that I have chosen for you. Turn to me and repent. And you will find grace sufficient to begin and sustain the change that I desire."

A hush fell over the crowd — did he mean for us to get down on our knees right now? Fr. Fullam stepped to the microphone. "I'd like each one of you to empty your hands, if you will, of whatever they contain. And I'd like to ask you to take your hands before you, something like this, and close your fists very tightly, until they hurt," and he extended his upturned fists in front of him. "And think, if you will, that in these hands you hold your life . . . If you find it in your heart tonight, to respond to the message that God has given us, I would ask you to slowly open those clenched fists with the hands and palms upward to the Lord, and let that simple act be the release of your life to the Lord . . ." And slowly he opened his fists, and forty thousand of us did likewise.

He prayed then, for all of us, asking the Lord to receive what we had given, to sanctify us by His Holy Spirit, and as we left, to fill our hearts with joy. "And now, as we go forth from this place, receive the blessing of God the Father, the Son, and the Holy Spirit. Let us go forth rejoicing in the power of the Spirit!" And so they did, with the same cheering and applause as before, just as if, I thought, the word of prophecy had never been spoken. The song being sung was the "Alleluia Song of Thanks," with its moving, Hebrew flavor, and its fast, upbeat tempo.

Up in the press box, Dean described for our transcribers back home what for us had become the most memorable image of the conference: "I wish you could see all these people, as they file out, dancing, singing the song that you can hear in the background, 'Alleluia'. On the stage, in the aisles, in the rows of seats, people are clapping their hands, dancing, arms locked together, swaying back and forth. In the end zone bleachers, whole sections of people have their arms raised and are waving them back and forth in time with the music — like the wind is sweeping through this big field of wheat . . . ."

But while Dean was caught up in the joy, I was concerned. It seemed to me that the repentance and brokenness which God had been calling for all conference long, in tender words at the beginning of this evening and with stern words at the end when it was not forthcoming, was still

Humble Yourselves Beneath My Hand 147

missing. I ran into Judy Tydings afterward, and mentioned it to her. "I wouldn't be too concerned about it," she smiled. "Once you've been to a few of these larger conferences, you'll come to see that the Holy Spirit has a way of working things out the way He wants them to. If something doesn't happen on one day, it will happen on another."

But neither of us could possibly have imagined how the Holy Spirit was about to work things out.

11

God's Leprechaun

It was past midnight by the time we had finally procured our homemade black cherry and mocha fudge ice cream cones at Topsy's, but as long as there were people gathered in the lobby of the Muehlebach, I didn't feel like going to bed. This night, there was a group of black Pentecostals standing and chatting with Vinson Synan, and since I knew him, I went over to join them. "What is this the press overhears about you having just been made a new bishop?" I asked Ithiel Clemmons. "Is that true, or are you an old bishop?"

"He's a new bishop; you're right," said Bishop S.L.Green from Chicago.

"Yes, I'm probably the newest member of the Board of Bishops," Ithiel Clemmons beamed. "It happened in April."

Speaking as a member of the planning committee, how did he feel that the conference was going? "There has been a breakthrough that has never been seen before. Tonight, on the podium, you saw Cardinal Suenens of the Catholic Church; Bishop J.O.Patterson, black Pentecostal; Tom Zimmerman, white Pentecostal; and all of them praising

God together — it's unbelievable! Ten years ago, it could not have happened."

And I thought to myself, as I stood in that circle with the Rev. Benny Ellison and Dr. James T. Watson of Chicago, and Dr. Theodore Tearose from Springfield, that our conversation was a mini-example of what he was talking about. We couldn't have come from more disparate backgrounds in America, but that really didn't matter, any more than the color of our skin. We all loved the Lord, and each in our own way was doing our best to serve Him — which gave us a great deal in common, after all.

Just as I was finally on my way to the elevator, I happened to cross David du Plessis' path. Having heard that he was flying out in the morning, after a session with the nondenominationals out at the Trade Mart, I took a chance and offered him a ride to the airport. He accepted with delight, remembering the last time I'd given him a ride — when a friend and I had met his plane, as he flew in from the Rome conference, in '75. We agreed that Dean and I would meet him at the Trade Mart a little after ten, and I went to bed, looking forward to sleeping in a little, for the first morning in what was beginning to seem like forever.

Sometime before the morning sun had done its thing, the phone rang. Muzzily I groped for it in the darkened room and answered it, trying to sound alert. It was David — could we also give him a ride from the Muehlebach to the Trade Mart? In about half an hour? Sure, I said cheerily, but inside my heart sank. That meant we would have to get up, get dressed and leave immediately. As soon as I hung up, I saw how far I had to go before I began to have the makings of a servant's heart. I was really disgusted with myself and asked the Lord to forgive me and give me a glad and grateful heart, which He did. And that morning turned out to be one of the most memorable highlights of the conference.

It was a glorious morning outside — clear and bright and a little cooler, for a change. We headed for the old municipal airport, with Dean navigating and David reminiscing. Listening to him, I was once more reminded of the extraordinary gift that he possessed for presenting Pentecost in the most disarming fashion, with a lively, self-deprecating, thoroughly appealing humor that encouraged men to laugh at their stuffiness and at the silly differences that kept them from coming together in the Spirit. He was old now, and he looked smaller than he used to — his face was seamed with many wrinkles, and his hair was snowy white. But his eyes were as bright as ever, and in them danced a mischievous twinkle. God's Leprechaun! And I thanked the Lord for what I sensed would be a memory that Dean and I would treasure for many years.

At the exhibition hall, the preliminary music had already begun, and the 2600 seats were filling fast. Up on the platform, eight musicians and singers were sounding like triple their number, as they performed a spirited rendition of "Sing to the Lord a New Song." In the audience, people were clapping time, and the joyous mood was positively infectious. It mattered not, how tired or grumpy or worried you were; that song on that morning, with the guitars and the whirling tambourines (I had never appreciated what a potent instrument the tambourine was, until I came to Kansas City) lifted you up out of whatever you might have been stuck in, and into the true joy of the Lord!

Judson Cornwall was the master of ceremonies this morning, and in order to give David time to catch his plane without feeling rushed, he re-arranged the morning's schedule, introducing him first, instead of last. Commenting on how seldom it was that a pioneer who had paid the price for progress lived to see the progress, Judson invited us all to join in prayer for David, who was very fatigued. We prayed, extending our hands towards him, and when he began to speak, all weariness slipped away, like an unwanted cloak. Doughty as ever, he spent the better part of an hour showing by his own example, how little difference there was, in the long run, between Classical, Neo and Catholic Pentecostals.

He reminded those present that Pope Paul in his Christmas message had appealed to *all* humanity to seek spiritual renewal. "Of course, the Protestants never thought they needed renewal, because they thought they were the renewal of the Catholic Church. And the Pentecostals didn't think *they* needed renewal, because they thought they were the renewal of the Protestant Church. But Pope John said, 'The *Church* needs renewal, and for this renewal there must be a new Pentecost.' And I said 'Isn't it amazing? God didn't say, "Come on, you old rascal, you think you're infallible." God used the Pope, in spite of the fact that Catholics believed he was infallible.'

"All of a sudden, the Evangelical Press Association gets a report that David has accepted the infallibility of the Pope as a dogma. I said, 'I didn't. I only said God is infallible, even if He uses the Pope.' " There was a burst of laughter, and I marveled at how deftly the Spirit used laughter to bring hearts together. David continued: "And I thank God for Pope John; he had the right spirit!" There was applause, but David wasn't finished. "Old Professor Barth [the great German theologian] used to say to me, and we had many wonderful encounters, 'David, you are excited about the ecumenical movement and the World Council; you wait till God moves the Catholics. Brother, then you'll see something!' And that was Karl Barth!"

With David, one good anecdote deserved another, and he told of a bishop saying to Barth, "You know, Pope John thinks very highly of you." To which Barth replied, "That's mutual; I think very highly of him." "Yes," the bishop said, "but he admitted that he thinks you are the greatest Protestant theologian in the world." David smiled, "and old Karl sat for a moment, and he said, 'So the Holy Father is infallible, after all!' " A roar of laughter filled the hall, followed by applause, then more laughter, and more applause.

There was a standing ovation for David at the end of his address, and it continued all the way out of the hall. On the way out, friends and well-wishers would lay a hand on his arm or say, "God bless you, David." And he would pause and nod and perhaps say a quick greeting and pat the hand resting on his arm. It occurred to me that in well over half a century of service, David must have made tens of thousands of such friends all over the world, perhaps three or four generations in the same family — people who loved him, and to whom he was — what? Not a patriarch, certainly; he would have shuddered at the word. Judson had called him a pioneer, and that was closer. What came to me, was a spiritual country doctor, whose homespun humor masked a reservoir of wisdom, and whose gentle, caring touch carried with it remarkable curative powers.

When we were in the car at last and headed for the airport, I told David that there was one episode which he had related to me when he had come back from Rome, and which I wished he would tell again. It was about the debate over the Virgin Mary, at the Vatican Council. He smiled at the memory and began. "At that council, there were 2200 bishops, 800 theologians, and one little Pentecostal — three thousand learned Catholics and me. The question had been placed on the agenda: should Mary be recognized as the Mother of the Church? And there, for more than a week, I heard the most astonishing arguments, pro and con, and finally one of the bishops, who was a chairman of one of the major committees, stood up and said, 'I cannot accept Mary as the Mother of the Church. All my life I have been taught that the Church is my mother and that God is the Father, and if Mary is now considered Mother of the Church, that will make her my grandmother!'

"Well, half the bishops roared with laughter, and the

other half gnashed their teeth, and I saw that the council was pretty evenly divided. The next thing we knew, Pope Paul had asked that the battle be stopped, and he had decided that she might be called Mother of the Church. And so they came to me, as they do with everything, and one asked, 'David, how do you feel about this? Can you accept Mary as Mother of the Church?' 'No,' I said, 'not yet.' 'Not *yet*? What do you mean?'

" 'Well, while you've been arguing, I've been studying the Word. And it's all right there. You know, I have the highest regard for Mary; she's the mother of my Lord.' And I said, 'Now, isn't Jesus the Bridegroom?' 'Yes.' 'And who's the Bride?' 'The Church.' 'Ah, but at the moment, they're still only engaged; after the Marriage Supper of the Lamb, Mary will be the mother-in-law of the Church!'

" 'Then you don't mind her being called the Mother of the Church?' 'Well, perhaps it is a bit premature, but I think we can forgive that; I mean, don't you know young fiancees who start calling their future mothers-in-law "Mother" before the wedding?'

"The bishop looked at me and said, 'I've never heard that before!' 'Neither have I,' I said, 'but I like it!' "

Dean and I both laughed. It seemed that God was using David to bring unity not only interdenominationally, but within the Catholic ranks, as well. "I've told that story many times to my Catholic friends," David admitted, "and when I went to Rome, Cardinal Suenens wanted to know how I could preach Mariology to meetings and have Catholics, Protestants and Pentecostals all shout Glory!"

We arrived at the airport in plenty of time. While Dean parked the car, I went with him while he made sure that his baggage, which had been sent out earlier, had been all checked in. As he opened his wallet, I was mildly surprised to note that there was only a single dollar in the fold, but I gave no thought to it, assuming that his expenses were well taken care of. Dean returned then, and we occupied three chairs in an out-of-the-way corner.

Speaking again of the Catholic Church, David exulted, because the Renewal had now leavened every one of the different orders, and initially there had been some concern that the Catholic Charismatics might form their own order. "I like this," said David, "because I find that in the Old Testament, God had one nation, Israel, for a witness, but he kept them twelve tribes forever. Only when they worshipped were they one nation; otherwise, in culture, in social life, they were, and are, twelve tribes to this day. If God was satisfied with that arrangement in the Old Testament, I think He will be quite happy to have all these denominational tribes, but when we worship, we must be one in the Spirit."

That seemed to me to be the best differentiation between unity and forced unanimity that I had yet heard. "And then in Revelation," David went on, "I find seven churches. And the Lord treated them as seven separate units, and He called them churches, plural. He never told one church to go and learn from another. He did not tell them to go form a society . . . He kept them like that, and each one was responsible for its own members . . . Here in Kansas City, we are *ten* tribes, ten different conferences, but as we came together in the stadium, there was only one conference!"

I liked the parallel. "It's a wonderful manifestation of unity — unity, in spite of our divisions. But I don't think they are divisions; I think God has permitted it to happen. I am an ecumaniac, and I believe in a Charismatic ecumenicity. That's why I'm so happy with this conference. Because I feel that here we have proved that we have no desire to pull out of our denominations. We intend to remain where we are, with each of us seeking to leaven our denominations."

David chuckled. "I always say, dynamite is for evangelizing the world, but in the Church, it's leaven that's needed, not dynamite. You blow up a church, and you can't get the pieces back together. Like that pastor I was talking to this morning. He had a large Baptist church, and when he came into the Baptism, some well-meaning Charismatic friends said to him, 'Now you've got the power; give it to them with both barrels!'

" 'So,' he said, 'I went into the pulpit, and I blasted them with both barrels. And one barrel blasted them out, and the other blasted me out, and now I have nothing.' I said to him, 'Be a doormat, and let them step on you and ask them to forgive you for your foolishness. Your friends that advised you knew nothing of pastoral duties. They don't understand that a pastor is a shepherd, and he doesn't beat the sheep; he leads them!' "

David spied one of the men he would be traveling with then, and we went over to get him settled away. I went to double-check the departure gate number, and soon we were waving goodbye, and I watched the small, white-haired figure walking down the boarding ramp.

12

The Sins of the Fathers

When we got back to Kansas City, Dean and I faced a couple of personal dilemmas, which, we later gathered, were fairly universal. First, though we had enough time for a fast lunch, there wasn't enough time for what we really wanted — a nap. And second, there were simply too many good workshops to choose from. It would take a month of afternoons, to take them all in! Over lunch we decided that Dean would cover the press conferences, while I felt I was supposed to go to the Messianic Jews' symposium at the Midland Theatre.

But then, instead of just being obedient to the leading of my heart, I started working the afternoon out in my head. Actually, the first part of their program was going to be Art Katz speaking on the holocaust, and since I had known Art personally for many years, I had heard him on that subject before. And meanwhile, Ken Pagard, of the planning committee, was going to be talking on developing Christian community, out at the Governor's Exposition Building, and Tom Smail, whom the Showalters had recommended, was holding a workshop in the gymnasium of the Cathedral of the Immaculate Conception . . . I could still catch that Jewish symposium and hang around afterwards to talk to the principals.

In the end, I decided that I'd better stay close to the center of town, and so did not hear Ken Pagard, though I later heard that he had had some excellent things to say. For instance, he made the point that the contemporary emphasis on individualism and independence was contrary to the whole purpose of God, pointing out that the works of Satan were always dividing, separating, disintegrating, and isolating, whereas the effect of God's work and activity was always bringing together and uniting, making a oneness. At the same time, he warned idealists and romantics to eschew community, explaining that in community the Holy Spirit worked on a very practical level in people's lives, as they rubbed against one another and had frustration and friction. But it was the cleansing they received, as they worked through these things, that helped them to grow spiritually.

Tom Smail was just wrapping up, when I finally found a parking place, and entered the gym. It was not air-conditioned, and must have been well over 90 degrees, so we went back to the Muehlebach and talked in his room. Tom was the head of the Fountain Trust in England now, having taken over that responsibility from Michael Harper, and he had come over for the conference, at the invitation of the Presbyterians. "Actually, they invited me for a month," he explained in his Scottish accent, "but we're having a similar conference ourselves in a week's time, in London. Not nearly so grand as this one — we're expecting around two thousand — but the Cardinal is coming, and Ken Pagard, and Sister Briege McKenna, and a lot of British people, as well."

What was the climate like for the Renewal on his side of the Atlantic? "I've found that the sort of problems and questions people are facing here are very much like the ones at home. What I found was a great desire to have the whole charismatic dimension related to the rest of the Gospel. They're slightly uncomfortable if it seems to be sitting on the side, and they don't know quite how to relate it to anything else. They become tremendously reassured, if you can relate the message of the Holy Spirit into the rest of it. And of course, the other thing in people's minds is, how it all gets integrated into the life of the churches."

Tom noticed that the red light on his phone was flashing, indicating there was a message for him; he excused himself and called for the message — someone wanting to see him before he left. "There's obviously been a lot more open opposition over here than we've encountered. What we run into is a lot of indifference and quite a lot of argument on the issues, but almost no ecclesiastical action to put Charismatic ministers out of the churches, or anything of the kind."

He looked out his window. "One of the big differences is that the Charismatics here are trying to penetrate a much more outwardly prosperous church situation than we have at home. Our churches have really been in a decline for some time, and when people are down on their beam ends, they're much more likely to look into the heart of the Gospel and see what they're missing. Whereas, if you've got lots of people and big programs and balanced budgets and whatnot, you can afford to shrug and say, 'We're fine as we are, why bother?'

"But," he slapped his knees briskly, "in England — and when I say England, I mean as opposed to Scotland, Ireland and Wales — I would say that the church situation is off bottom again, and on the way up. Particularly in the Church of England, and among the Baptists. These are the two groups that are being the most affected by the Renewal. And now, of course, the Catholics."

What for him personally had been the highlight of the conference? "In the particular conference I've been in, there's been a real dovetailing of ministries — Catherine Marshall, Rod Williams and I have found ourselves saying, 'Has he or she been looking at my notes?' because we've been coming out with the same sort of things. It gives you the feeling that the Spirit's been around."

Was there anything else of significance that he had noted? He rubbed his chin. "I do think it's significant that there's been very little emphasis on just the spiritual gifts alone. I mean, it's very much a *Christian* renewal movement. The emphasis has been on the whole life of Christ . . . You think of Arrowhead, and you think of ecumenism, holiness, fellowship — the Renewal has grown beyond its very early stages, when people tended to get excited and perhaps over-concentrated on particular spiritual gifts."

I thanked Tom very much then, and started for the Midland Theatre. But sitting on the stairs to the mezzanine, facing the Wyandotte exit, were Ralph Martin and Bruce Yocum. I thanked the Lord for that happy coincidence, because up to that moment, Ralph had not been at all visible, except in the Word Gifts Group, of which Bruce was the leader and he a member. Reading *Fire on the Earth*, I had formed a mental image of him which, as usual, did not exactly jibe with reality. He was shorter than I expected, and a good deal younger-looking. But the most striking feature about him was his eyes — they were sort of gray-green, and I had the feeling that he saw much more than he spoke.

What did he see that was worthy of note about the conference? "People in quite different segments of the Body of Christ are sensing that there is a unity among them . . . . Groups which have a very small representation here are beginning to hear something that's going to enable them to go back to their people and say, 'The Lord is doing something new. We've got to open up to it. We've got to see it.' "

What personally had given him the most joy about the conference? He thought for a while, before answering. "Seeing the leaders from the different segments of the Body of Christ really being touched by the Lord, and their hearts opening up to one another and to Him . . . When I see God touching the leaders, I know it's just the beginning!"

I suddenly realized how late it was getting, and took my leave. In spite of the beautifully simple map on the back of the program, I got lost on the way to the Midland. When I finally arrived, I was startled to find that instead of a symposium in progress, there seemed to be complete disorder. A great many people were coming up on the stage and going down, and the Jewish leaders, one of them in his undershirt, were either talking to them or to one another. And yet, amidst this apparent chaos, there was that same strong sense that God had done something important, that I had felt the day before in Bartle Hall. I asked a man standing at the back of the theatre what was going on.

"You weren't here?" he said, almost as a rebuke, and I was instantly reminded of the leading I had originally gotten — and had chosen to modify and devalue. "Boy," he said, shaking his head, "you really missed something!"

"What?" I persisted, getting a little annoyed — and increasingly convicted.

"Well, Arthur Katz just blew the lid off! He said that the Jews were responsible for Christ's death, and because they had refused to accept that responsibility, they had reaped the Holocaust. When he finished, one of the other leaders called for a basin with water and a towel, and two other leaders started washing Katz's feet. Then Jews came onto the stage to stand and accept the forgiveness of the Catholics in the audience, and the Catholics asked forgiveness of the Jews, and some of them washed the Jews' feet, and now healing lines have formed — it's fantastic!"

I nodded and somewhat dazed made my way down front. I had never heard Art speak of the Holocaust like *that* before! And who should be standing beside the stage, changing film, but our photographer, John Sorensen!

"You were here for the whole thing?" I asked him incredulously.

"Yup," he said. "Got some good pictures, too."

As much as I wanted to hear his account of what had happened, I wanted even more to know how, out of twenty-eight workshops, he had happened to be at this one. "That's a story in itself," he replied. "I'd spent the last part of the morning running around, taking pictures of that procession of Catholic priests through the center of town. There must have been a couple of hundred of them, in their white robes, with traffic cops holding back cars at the intersections... Anyway, I was running after them, taking pictures, and then running to the front of the column to take more, and it was hot out there! This bag," he indicated the leather satchel he carried his equipment in, "must weigh twenty pounds. By one o'clock, I was headed for the hotel room, to get off my feet."

He shook his head at the memory of what happened next. "As I was walking along, I noticed that the man next to me had a white cane, so when we came to the corner, I asked him if I could help him across the street. He said yes, and took my arm, and I figured, well, I might as well see him one more block. We got to talking, and I asked him where he was going, and he said, 'To hear Arthur Katz.' I said, 'Oh, where's that?' and he said it was two blocks down and then over one, and the theatre was on the right — he had the whole city memorized and could have made it without any help. But I walked along with him anyway.

"Each block, I thought, well, I'll just leave him and go back to the hotel now, but somehow I just didn't. When we got to the theatre, there was a long waiting line, so I waited with him, thinking, 'I'll just get him a good seat where he can hear everything and then take a few pictures and leave.' I found him a seat and checked the layout of the place for the best shooting angles and where the most available light was, and went and got permission — and never left." He stopped. "Hey, what's the matter with you?" he said, looking at me.

"Oh, nothing," I lied. When one person, whom God

wants to be in a certain place at a certain time, or to speak a certain word, refuses to be obedient to His leading, I thought, then God will find another person who will be obedient, to take his place. And how like God, to use a blind man (or angel?) to do it.

"Well, tell me what happened," I said to John brightly, though bright was the last thing I felt.

"Ray Gannon, who was scheduled to speak before Katz, couldn't be here — his wife is having a baby — so an Assemblies of God preacher who was a friend, read a synopsis of his speech, which took about fifteen minutes and gave Arthur Katz maybe twenty minutes more than he would have had otherwise. And he needed every minute of it.

"The synopsis of Gannon's speech placed the blame for the Holocaust on the Church's historic attitude towards the Jews, and the Church was going to have to face up to this, because it couldn't be cleansed and healed, until it was dealt with. But that wasn't the way Katz saw it. *He* said that the Jews had no one but themselves to blame, because they had never faced up to the fact that they had put their Messiah on the Cross!"

John warmed to his subject. "You really should have been here! Katz started off with some nice, ingratiating remarks of the kind that bring applause, but then he asked them to hold their applause until the end, warning them that by the time he got finished, they might not feel like applauding. He said that the Lord had sat him down in his hotel room for eight hours and would not let him up until he had written down what he was now going to read. He had written it on yellow legal paper, and had not corrected it or even looked at it until now." John paused. "You're really going to have to get a tape of his speech as soon as you can and listen to it."

Well, what happened after that? "He gave an altar call of sorts, unlike any I'd ever heard of. First, he asked any

The Sins of the Fathers

Gentiles in the audience who had any heaviness in their hearts where the Jews were concerned, and who would be free from the burden of guilt for the sins of their fathers, to stand up where they were. And then he invited the Jews in the audience to come forward and stand facing the others, and each group to extend their arms towards one another, while he led them in a prayer of repentance and forgiveness, forgiving each other, and asking the Lord's forgiveness for their own sin. Because whether it was the Crucifixion or the Holocaust, no one here was without sin."

David Stern made an announcement then, appealing for people to leave the theatre, but no one made a move towards the exit. "The most amazing thing of all happened next," John continued. "People started experiencing healing all over the place, and little groups formed. I don't know what they were saying, but you could tell that they were getting reconciled, and deep ethnic hurts were being healed. And then another Jewish leader, Mike Evans, announced that they'd sent for a basin and water and towels, and that they wanted a representative from each of the different denominations to come up on stage, so that the Jews could wash their feet. But first the Jews started washing each other's feet, telling the others that they could not call anyone else to repentance, until they had first repented themselves, as the day before there'd been a lot of sharp, open dissension among the leaders.

"By this time the program was out the window, but everyone seemed to know that the Holy Spirit had taken over. And this foot-washing wasn't gimmicky or contrived. This was the Holy Spirit, and the whole thing flowed beautifully. Oh, and I got some good pictures, too."

As soon as I could, I listened to a tape of the speech which had triggered it all. Art wasted no time getting to the point. "Among my burdens is the burden for repentance. And I have been grieved at the absence of this great theme in modern evangelism . . . May I suggest that there is no faith toward Jesus Christ, until there is first repentance toward God." And he swiftly moved to confront the Jewish conscience from Scripture: "Therefore, let all the house of Israel know assuredly that God hath made the same Jesus whom you have crucified, both Lord and Christ. Now when they heard this, they were pricked in their hearts, and said unto Peter and the rest of the apostles, 'Men and brethren, what shall we do?' Then said Peter unto them, 'Repent...'" (Acts 2:36-38).

As I listened, I had to remind myself that this was a converted Jew, confronting his own race. If he had preached thus in ancient Israel, they would have stoned him to death! He moved on to prick the hearts and consciences of all Charismatics. "I see the dove of God everywhere celebrated... but I have to note the absence of the Cross of Christ Jesus in our Charismatic conferences. I think it is Basilea Schlink who says that the great calamity of the Church has been its failure to prepare God's people for suffering. God did not give us His Spirit just to jazz up our denominational life. He gave Him to us, to equip us at the end of the age to stand and to serve God in hard places."

Returning to his main theme, he reminded the Jews of the oath that their fathers shouted at Pilate: " 'His blood be upon us *and upon our children!*' The magnitude of the horror of contemplating the Holocaust as a fulfillment of these words is so great, even for us who believe, that we shrink from its consideration... We Jews are as unwilling to face the implications of that, as Germans are to face the implications of the Holocaust. And the reason is the same. A concealed lie, hidden and ignored, mounts and becomes too hideous to examine. If we but once acknowledge *that*, what about the rest of our lies and deceptions? The whole foundation of our false life topples. All is vain; *we are undone!*

"You know what I say to that? *Hallelujah!* Because the collapse will bring the contrition and repentance that David sang of, and after it, deep conversion, and then will come the cry of God, 'Who will go for me?' And send us He will, in the name of the Lord, in the way of brokenness and humility, without the characteristic arrogance and disdain that marks the Jewish attitude towards Gentiles, whose feet we are now ready to wash. For he who has been much forgiven, loves much.

"And," he concluded, "they shall obtain joy and gladness, for sorrow and sighing shall pass away. I have been a critic of the Charismatic technique and manipulation of feigning joy by repeated choruses. Children, joy in the spontaneous overflow of the truly redeemed heart that has recognized its terrible transgressions against God, and has received total forgiveness and release."

He closed with two prayers. He absolved the Gentiles, in the name of Jesus, of the guilt and implications in the crimes of their fathers against the Jewish people. And then for the Jews who had never acknowledged for themselves the sins of their fathers who had "rejected your word in every manner that you sent it, through the prophets, through Moses, the written word, and the Word made flesh," he also prayed. "Lord, we ask you to forgive our cowardly hearts that would have chosen Barabbas rather than Jesus. And now we choose you again, Lord, and affirm our standing with you. And we are willing by that also to suffer all reproach in calling men to a true reckoning, to a true repentance, to a true conversion."
And he asked forgiveness and the blood-washing, in Jesus' name.

When it was over, I just sat there, stunned.

Mike Evans later told me what happened next. "As I went to announce the symposium that was to follow, the Lord spoke in a very strong voice within me and said *No.* I just stood there, trembling, and wondering what in the world did He mean by that? And then He said we were to have a foot-washing. Now. I glanced at the other leaders;

there was no time to discuss it with them, much less submit it to them. So, literally in fear and trembling, I asked one of the brothers to fetch basin, towels and water. My voice was shaking, because where would he find such things in a theatre? But if it was God telling me, then God would show him where to find them. We sang 'He is Lord' then, and before we had finished, the brother was coming down the aisle, bearing the items I'd asked for.

"We set them before a chair in the middle of the stage. Art sat in the chair, and two of the other leaders, Manny Brotman and Moishe Rosen, knelt and started washing his feet and ministering to him and praying for him. Within moments, the Spirit of God blew through the entire place, and more than a thousand people were weeping and travailing before God, and reconciling themselves. All the Jewish leaders were now ministering and praying and weeping over one another, as God seemed to break all of our hearts.

"The Catholic priests started coming up, sharing that they felt a necessity to wash the feet of the Jews, and the Jewish leaders washed *their* feet, and on and on it went." (Later, when I shared this with Harry Lunn, one of our Kansas City helpers, it recalled an incident that had occurred nine years before, during the pontificate of John XXIII. A delegation of rabbis from Israel arrived at the Vatican, and instead of having them brought to him, Pope John went to the waiting room, embraced each with a kiss of peace, and said, 'I am Joseph, the brother.')

"In the midst of all this," continued Mike, "a man came forward and told us that his uncle had been a member of Hitler's General Staff and had been responsible for the deaths of tens of thousands of Jews, and he carried great guilt over this. He wanted to be reconciled, and we felt that we were to wash his feet and minister to him, as Jewish leaders.

"And now the Lord gave instruction for all present to

remove their shoes, and we sang and worshiped Him and wept together for about an hour. Then the Lord seemed to indicate that healing lines might form, and one of the Jewish leaders was standing there in his undershirt; he had used his shirt to wash someone's feet."

And that was where I had come in. Two other comments we received the next day helped to put it in perspective. David Stern, the Messianic Jewish representative on the planning committee, said, "Jesus said that one is to bring forth fruit and acts meet for repentance. Foot-washing is only a symbolic act . . . Only if the symbolic gets expressed in something real, does any good come out of it. And I mean that, not only in relation to the Gentiles washing the Jews' feet, and the Jews washing the Gentiles' feet, but also in relation to the Jewish leaders washing each other's feet. That, too, is a symbolic act. When people have different ministries, different attitudes as to how things should be done, and they are constantly in relationship to one another, caring for those relationships is an ongoing affair. It isn't taken care of in an afternoon of footwashing, or an afternoon of anything else."

Matt Schwartz seemed to sum it up for everyone: "You know, there's been a real sense of being one in the Spirit during this whole conference. But there needs to be a oneness of soul, like a brotherhood being formed, the knitting together of our lives in real, practical ways. I think, in terms of Jewish and Gentile oneness, there has been a real looking to the Lord, a coming here in vision, receiving life from Jesus together. But the deep, deep things that have been in the souls of the Gentiles over the centuries towards the Jews, and the deep things inside the Jewish soul — something of that was really released, a breaking, a cleansing, a healing, a knitting, especially in the lives of those who came forward. And in my own life, something deep within my soul was coming out. I found myself being joined to those people who were washing my feet, or whose feet I was washing."

Michael Scanlan

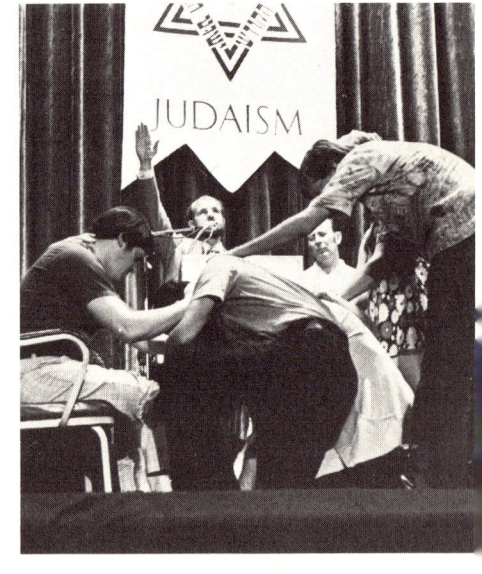

Terry Fullam

Ralph Martin, prophesying

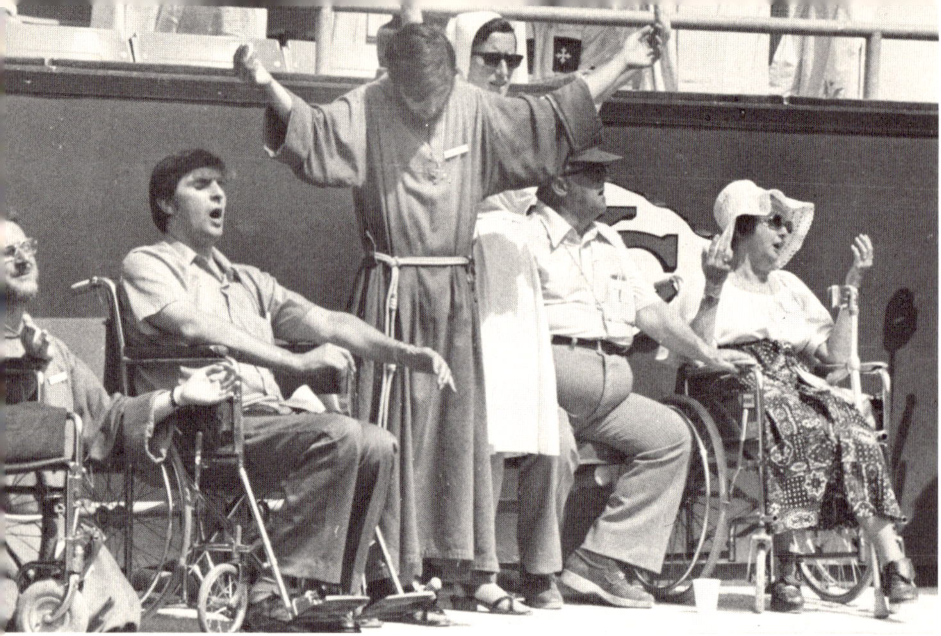

WE ARE
GOD BLESSED
SPIRIT POWERED
CHRIST CENTERED
ANGEL GUARDED
AMEN
FORD

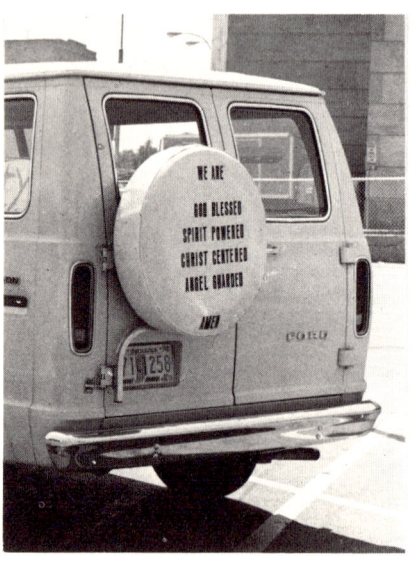

13

Faith-building

Walking out of the Midland Theatre that Saturday afternoon was like walking into a warm damp blanket. As much as I would have liked to make my way very slowly up to the Muehlebach, so as not to be soaked by the time I got there, I couldn't. It was twenty to five, and I had an interview with Francis MacNutt in five minutes. Even hurrying, I was three minutes late when I knocked on his door. But fortunately, some movie people were with him at the time, so he didn't notice.

I should not have been surprised to find that, up close, he had every bit as much charisma as he did as a small figure in white down on the speakers' platform. But I was. With his six-foot-plus stature, broad shoulders, chiseled features and iron grey hair, he looked like Charlton Heston might have looked, had he become a priest, instead of an actor.

What about that incredible healing service yesterday morning at Bartle Hall? Had he noticed anything from the platform that we down on the floor might have missed?

"Well, since healing is a large part of our ministry, I'm always especially aware of the different levels at which people operate. I've gotten very used to something which surprised me at first: you get a whole group of people who all look like they're wildly happy and praising God and everything, and yet underneath, there's this other thing — this anguish — going on all the time. And it's the same, wherever you go; underneath this fantastic rejoicing, there are people suffering, even though they themselves might be joining in. And the happier the others get, the more left out the ones who are hurting feel. And although they're afraid to say it in the group, you can see it in their eyes. And then privately they'll come up and say, 'I'm falling apart; please pray for me.' So you have that double movement all the time — the general rejoicing and the deeper, hidden agenda of those people who are suffering."

I asked him then, since he was one of the members of the Word Gifts Group, if it had seemed to him that the Lord had been calling for repentance the past two evenings and had expressed His impatience in the final prophecy of last night.

"Well, I feel the most comfortable myself with something where it's not set up too much beforehand, but look at just the logistics problems in dealing with such a huge crowd . . . And then you're dealing with people who are in union but who have never worked together before, who probably met each other for the first time on the platform that night — how do you deal with that? I spoke on healing Thursday night, and a lot of people said afterwards that they sensed the leading, when I finished, was to get out there and really start praying for healing. But that would have completely broken up what was to come afterwards, like you have Ruth, and especially Larry Christenson, who got on so late as it was, that it was unfair to him. And so to follow then what seemed to be the movement of the Spirit would have wrecked what was planned."

He stretched his long frame in the chair and smiled. "It doesn't upset me too much. I *was* conscious of that last night, and I didn't see any point where anybody could have called to repentance in any kind of realistic way. There was no point where I felt the Lord saying, 'Now is the time to say that.' So maybe it was for a future time . . .'' He gazed out the window at the late afternoon sky.

"And regarding what happened Thursday night, maybe it was better the way it worked out. Because the Methodists had a healing service, and we had one, and the Episcopalians had one . . . and there was probably a whole lot more individual attention that was given at those sessions than would have been the case out at Arrowhead. Maybe it was better to have it put on hold overnight . . ."

It was five-fifteen and time to head for Arrowhead. I had reserved the wagon for my own use this afternoon, in the hopes of offering Fr. MacNutt a ride and thereby extending the interview. But he was waiting to go out with some others, so I thanked him and headed for the garage. I had just left the elevator, when I happened to pass Ruth Stapleton, unaccompanied for a change. I had tried a couple of times since my tongue-tied fiasco, to talk to her, but she had been tied up. Now I got a nudge to ask her one more time. I didn't want to risk being turned down again, but even more I didn't want to risk ignoring the leading of the Spirit, so I asked her. "Why, sure," she said, and we sat down on one of the sofas in the lobby. Beautiful under any circumstances, this afternoon she was positively radiant with joy at what the Holy Spirit had done in her workshop and was delighted to have the opportunity to share it. The workshop had been out at the Trade Mart, and she was sharing it with Herman Riffel, a Baptist minister from Michigan. They had arranged to take turns speaking, he first, then she, after which they would also take turns ministering. But she had gotten held up in traffic, with the result that he took the first hour alone.

"So when I got up, he had really laid the groundwork, the Scriptural basis for the workshop. I made a few comments to tie it all in, but before I could start the prayer for inner healing, people started crying all over the place, and there must have been close to three thousand, all told. I called on all the ministers who had worked in inner healing to please come and help, and so maybe fifteen came up and started going to different people. One or two were having really intense pain, so I asked them to take these out and for the rest of the group to just pray and remain quiet in prayer.

"When I finally got started into the prayer, there was an anointing the likes of which I have never seen, with the exception of the first workshop we did at Notre Dame. I asked again for help, and about a hundred more ministers came up and went into all parts of the auditorium. What caused all the emotion to come up was when I said, 'Just imagine Jesus holding you, and allow all of your hurts to come into His healing love and be consumed by His love . . . .'

"As time went on, Herman Riffel, the minister who was working with me, sent a note: 'Don't stop. Forget the program. Keep on going.' So when it got so intense that I could hardly stand up, the power was so great, I asked him if he would come and let me lean on his arm. The whole thing was so draining that without him, I don't think I could have stood. But he stood with me until we got to the very end.

"I didn't feel that I was going to be able to get everything back together, but the Lord was faithful, and the Spirit really began to minister peace. Some people even began to laugh —"

"That's beautiful!" I exclaimed.

"Oh, I wish you could have seen it!" Ruth replied, her eyes shining. "There was no unfinished work; all the people, even the ones who had been so emotional, were laughing and praising the Lord! So we ended with a praising time, and I shook everybody's hand and now," she laughed, "I can hardly move my fingers, they squeezed so hard."

I thanked her, and as I climbed the steps towards the Wyandotte exit, I was filled with awe at the forgiving mercy of God, who had not only redeemed my elevator cop-out but provided a far better interview than I could ever have gotten before! Passing through the revolving door, I noticed Fr. Mike Scanlan waiting there and looking at his watch. I glanced at my own; it was a quarter to six and getting late, so on a hunch, I asked him if he wanted a ride. He hesitated, then asked if I had room for another priest Fr. Francis Martin. I said sure, and soon we were en route for Arrowhead.

Fr. Mike was president of the College of Steubenville and chairman of the Catholic Service Committee, so I was looking forward to talking to him, convinced that the Holy Spirit had arranged yet another 'coincidence'. So I was disappointed when Fr. Mike, who was one of the featured speakers that night, said that he would like to use the ride out for a little quiet time with the Lord.

To pass the time, I asked Fr. Martin, a very soft-spoken, unassuming man in his forties, where he was from. It turned out that he taught Talmudic literature at the Ecole Biblique in Jerusalem, where he was also finishing his doctoral thesis. What was more, he taught the Talmud in the Aramaic translations that Jesus himself would have heard. But it wasn't until he mentioned that he came from a community in Canada, that I suddenly began paying close attention. What was the name of the community? "Madonna House. Did you ever hear of a book called *Poustinia*?" I assured him that I had. "Well, that's my community."

"You're kidding! I live in a community on Cape Cod, and that book was practically required reading for us a few years ago! So, you're looking forward to going home, eh?"

"Yes, if that's what I'm supposed to do, when I've finished."

We talked about community for a while, then I asked him

what would be the most lasting impression of living in Jerusalem that he would take back with him. "The grace of living there — because somehow it's still a place where God is and moves in mysterious ways. It is living where all the issues that make up world history are distilled . . . There are the Jews and the Muslims, who hate one another, and we Christians are in the minority, as we are in the world in general . . . On that level, you see the world situation; on another level, the Word of God comes without any frills — you either buy it with all the consequences, or you do something else."

We were pulling into Arrowhead, as Fr. Mike, whom I had thought to be praying or dozing or both, spoke for the first time: "Why don't you tell him about your association with Cardinal Suenens?"

My curiosity was aroused — what was the connection? "Well, I've known Cardinal Suenens for about sixteen years; in fact, I've translated most of his writings that have appeared in English. And when the Renewal began, I wrote him and said, 'You know, I really think that of everything the Lord has done in your life, this is where it's at.' Then in 1971, I was in Rome, starting my research, and when the Cardinal came to Rome to see the Pope, he got in touch. 'Here I am,' he said. 'Now what are you talking about?'

"So we talked, and I explained — he had already had contact, you know. He had been to the States the year before, and knew that the Renewal existed. I had encouraged him to visit Ann Arbor and Houston, and he did .

Anyway, we were giving some lectures together in Brussels. My first talk was on discerning ministries, and he sat in the front row like a schoolboy, you know, asking questions, 'What do you think of that?' and 'Would you say this?' And that was the night, in his chapel, that we prayed for the Baptism in the Holy Spirit."

We had arrived at the parking lot, and we all needed to get inside quickly. As we got out of the car, I glanced over at Fr. Mike in mute appreciation for his having asked if Fr. Francis might join us; it had indeed been one of God's 'coincidences,' after all. Fr. Mike shrugged and smiled. "You and I can talk after I get done speaking tonight. I'll have a better idea of what I want to say then, anyway."

I nodded and hurried to find Dean. We had an interview with Bob Mumford scheduled for six, and it was after that now. Checking the press room, I learned that the press conference in the game-film room was still in progress. That's where he would be, and I was about to leave to get the elevator, when I happened to glance at the photo table, where new photos were put out for reporters who wanted to order them. There, on top of the selection, was a group photo of a dozen people or so, including two faces which I recognized: Hal Helms, from our community, and Dave Emmons, who was with our contingent in Kansas City. What were they doing in a photograph in the press room, I thought, as I rode down in the elevator? It wasn't just a casual, people shot; they were much too self-conscious for that . . . Well, I didn't have time to worry about that now.

In the game-film room, I found Dean with a number of the press, listening to a Kansas City friend of ours, Warren Black. What was *he* doing, talking to the press corps? But that was another question that would have to go unanswered. Quickly conferring with Dean, we agreed that he would stick with the press conference, and I would talk to Bob alone.

I met Bob in the little restaurant where the speakers could be alone together before the evening's program, and we decided to hold our interview in the coaches' dressing room. On our way there, as we walked around the outside of the stadium, up on the fifth level, he asked me how the book project was shaping up. I told him, adding with a laugh that I had given up my anxiety and now had the faith to believe that God would finish what He had begun.

Bob took me by the arm then, and said, "I just want you

to know that if you boys do run short, I want to help you in any way that I can, and I mean even digging into my own pocket —"

"Thanks, Bob," I murmured, barely able to speak. And as we walked along, I looked out at the trees in the distance, so that he wouldn't see how moved I was. Though we had not previously met, Bob and I had strong differences of opinion. And those differences were not resolved. I still felt the same way, and he did, too, and we both knew it. But I also knew what my heart was telling me: that his concern was genuine and his offer sincere. My eyes brimmed at the thought of it. Regardless of our differences, from that moment on, Bob Mumford was my brother in Christ.

Our interview was almost academic after that. I had to ask him something, so I asked him what it had been like to be on the planning committee. "It's been a long and demanding experience," he admitted, "but never in my life have I worked with a committee of men from different denominations, where there's been such an absence of politics, jealousy and competition. Almost from the beginning, there was a sense of destiny and excitement, and a tremendous yielding to one another. And this was at the level where the problems usually are, though they're not discussed outside. But that sense of love and commitment to one another at the planning committee level is what gave us the courage to really believe — I mean deeply heartbelieve — that God wanted to do something in Kansas City."

And part of what He wanted to do, I thought to myself, I had just experienced in a deep and personal way, thanks to Bob Mumford. The Word Gifts Group was beginning to gather across the hall; I thanked Bob and we went our separate ways — separate, but not separated.

When I told Dean what had happened, he was as moved as I had been, and then he had some pretty exciting news, too. At the last press conference, they had just announced the birth of two new charismatic fellowships. One was made up of members and former members of holiness churches — the Church of the Nazarene, the Wesleyan Church, the Church of Christ and Christian Union, the Free Methodist Church, the Church of God, Anderson, Indiana, and the Christian and Missionary Alliance. (So *that* was what Warren Black, whom I knew to be a Nazarene, was doing: briefing the press corps!)

"The other fellowship is of the United Church of Christ," Dean added, "and guess what? Hal and Dave Emmons have been elected to the steering committee!" (Which explained the photograph!)

Dean went on to fill me in on the earlier press conferences with representatives from the different denominations. They covered mostly familiar ground, but Dean felt that some of the remarks, which he had taped, might be worthy of note. He was right. In the first conference, a member of the secular press asked about the increasingly ominous endtime prophecies that were being received in the Charismatic fellowships of different denominations. Kevin Ranaghan fielded that one. "I can speak for the Catholic Service Committee, in the sense that we, too, sense as a body that we are, in fact, moving into times of difficulty, to times of deprivation and persecution. This is something we have arrived at in terms of spiritual discernment, but you can look in the writings of many futurists, sociologists, economists, and political scientists, and see the same kind of handwriting on the wall. Now in that kind of situation, it's especially important for Christians to be solid with one another, for the sake of the Body of Christ in times of difficulty, and for the sake of evangelization — in building up the Body of Christ, and expanding the Kingdom of God, in such times."

I was coming to have a far greater appreciation of the value of press conferences. Some deliberately tough questions were being asked by the secular press, and it was encouraging to see how deftly the Holy Spirit was providing the answers. I had no doubt that those Christians present but not actually speaking were praying for those on the firing line.

Out of that first conference also came the best definition I'd yet heard of where the Charismatic Renewal was at. It was given by Larry Christenson: "If you were holding this press conference ten years ago, you would have been hearing many expressions describing a sort of personal, spiritual awakening, very much in a vertical direction, of one's own relationship with Christ. But today, I think you're picking up very much of a horizontal kind of thing. This is not neglecting the vertical, but rather growing out of it — committed relationships, community, a sense of the growing oneness of the Body of Christ. This has been the direction the Renewal has taken in recent years, a growth toward a greater understanding of inter-personal relationships and the centrality of covenant love in Christian communities. To me, that's an indication that the Renewal is moving toward a greater witness for Christ in a corporate way, rather than simply as individuals."

In the second conference, Ralph Martin was thrown an obviously loaded question by one woman reporter: "I wonder if you would tell us exactly what the Charismatic movement is doing to improve on the general position and Dogma and teaching of the Roman Catholic Church?"

Ralph thought a moment. "I would say that the Charismatic movement is helping Catholics to live the essence of their faith, which is basic Christianity; it's helping them to love God and love their neighbor and —"

"But haven't they always tried to do that?" the reporter cut in. "How is the movement changing doctrine?"

"The Charismatic Renewal isn't particularly changing doctrine. It's helping people to live, in this day and age, the basic Christian doctrine which the Catholic Church has held for two thousand years. Now one of the things it's doing," Ralph added, trying to give the reporter a specific answer to her question, "is maybe helping Catholics to get some perspective on what's really the central thing, and what are more secondary things, like it's certainly helping Catholics to recognize the centrality of the person of Christ, and they're seeing Mary and the saints as, you know, part of the whole picture, but not the center..."

Another reporter, also a woman, asked Maria von Trapp: "When you were speaking at the stadium, you could have said anything you wanted to; why did you tell us about husbands and wives and speak against Women's Lib?"

"Because I was free to say anything I wanted, and this is clearly what is on my heart, on my soul, and right outside here on my lips. Women's Lib is doing a great damage to mothers and housewives, making them feel inferior and not want to be that anymore. Look how it helps the breakdown of family life in America. We are here since 1938, one generation. When we came, there was a strong sense of family life in this country. We gave two thousand concerts in those early years, and many, many times we were invited after the concert into a family home, and invariably they would say, 'Well, we sing together also. We stand around the piano, and we sing, and at Christmas time we sing carols, every free evening.' But that's almost gone. Hardly anybody's doing things together anymore. A family is now a group of people living under the same roof, each one comes and goes.... And Women's Lib is encouraging housewives and mothers to leave their homes, and belittling what they've been doing."

Another reporter addressed a question to planning committee member Judson Cornwall: "A person getting involved in the Charismatic Renewal — should he stay in the church or leave to a free church system?"

"I strongly urge everyone to stay in their church. I'm convinced that the Holy Spirit has come first to the individual, and if that individual can help renew another, they can eventually renew the church . . . When asked, 'How long must I stay in the church?' I've strongly suggested that they should stay until they get the left foot of fellowship — a euphemism for being thrown out. As long as they'll have them, let them stay. But we also caution them not to try to make the others Charismatic; just share the life, and let Christ be there."

"Reverend Cornwall," someone else asked, "if the Charismatic move of this past ten years is designed to bring all churches together as you earlier seemed to indicate, how come the independent Charismatics are having a double conference this week?"

"I think perhaps you may have overstated my concept. I don't think the Charismatic Renewal has come to make all churches one. I think it has come to bring a unity among the churches. We're going to be separate all the way to heaven, and I think there are a few groups who won't go, if they can't be assured of a separate berth when they get there. But there *is* a new unity in spirit. When I announced this morning to the 'A' nondenominationals that we were going to have a joint communion service tomorrow with the 'B' nondenominationals, there was a standing ovation."

Someone addressing Ralph Martin said that Cardinal Suenens had given the impression that in Europe the Renewal is regarded as a strictly American phenomenon.
"Okay, speaking in terms of the Catholic Renewal, since the Rome conference in '75, when the Pope gave us his blessing, there's been a real change in attitude. In Belgium, we have been deluged with requests from all over Europe to help and assist them in moving forward in the Renewal and moving towards community. The growth varies greatly from country to country. For example, in Ireland, it's growing very rapidly: more than twenty percent of the Irish nuns and ten per cent of the Irish priests are involved in the Renewal. In France, there's over sixty thousand Catholics

involved in the Renewal, with a strong ecumenical dimension in the south of France, where most of the Protestants are. There's a strong commitment on the part of Catholic and Protestant leaders to really move together, and that's quite a thing, because of the history of the persecution of the Huguenots and the Protestants in France. In Italy, since the Rome conference, there's been a very rapid growth, and it's just starting to take off in Spain . . ."

Dean nudged me and nodded in the direction of the door. Paul De Celles, the overall coordinator for the People of Praise, had just come in. We went up to him and asked if we might talk to him for a moment, and he agreed, adjourning with us across the hall to the coaches' dressing room.

What could he tell us about the original decision to put on the conference? "When it came to the question of putting this conference on, and we began to see what was involved financially, we realized that if we made mistakes, we would bankrupt the CRS and the People of Praise. So the question was: should we take the risk? And at various stages along the way, we felt like there was a fifty-fifty chance that it would fail . . . We certainly had full confidence in the planning committee, but we were well aware that if they went bankrupt first, we would be bankrupt finally. And so, we really had to lay it on the line — and we had to do so, time and time again. It's been a real walk of faith."

We thanked Paul and rejoined the Word Gifts Group, where there was a palpable sense of anticipation. The Lord was clearly going to do something of surpassing importance tonight, but none of the prophecies seemed to indicate exactly what. As tired as both Dean and I were, our fatigue seemed to fall away, as we sensed the awesomeness of God's being about to work His purpose out.

Just as the Word Gifts Group left the room to file out

onto the field, I saw Brick Bradford in the hallway and stopped to talk to him, while Dean went up to the press box, to cover the opening of the evening's program. What had the conference done in or for Brick personally? "It's been a real faith-builder, Dave. Having been on the planning committee for almost two years and watched this develop from its embryo stage, it's really raised my vision of what can occur as Christians work together. When we began to reflect, for example, on just how much this was going to cost — over $900,000 — we saw that we were laying our reputations and everything else on the line. I mean, how could we ever underwrite it? Well, the conference was not our doing, but the Lord's doing; if we were doing the will of God, He always pays for what He orders. Consequently, we finally released the whole thing to Him. After all, if we were in His will, there was no need to be so uptight about it."

I hear you, Lord, I thought to myself. I thanked Brick and hurried to join Dean in the press box for the opening of the final evening program. And suddenly it struck me that it *was* the final evening. By this time tomorrow, it would be all over, and that thought somehow made me very sad.

14

The Victor King

It was twenty after seven when I got to the press box. Dean was there, saying goodbye to Pete and Francois, as the latter would be flying out in the morning. I was glad to have gotten there in time to say goodbye myself, for although we had known each other only a few days and could hardly speak each other's language, the Lord had forged a bond of friendship between us. I looked out at all the people settling into their seats and beginning to sing, and wondered how many other similar friendships He had forged.

After Francois and Pete left, I went down on the field, to be at the heart of what the assembly was feeling, this final night. Walking out to where the cameramen were clustered in front of the speakers' platform, I joined the last strains of "Sing to the Lord a New Song" which had become a conference favorite. I sensed that there were many besides myself who felt a light sadness at the thought that this would be our last night at Arrowhead, that by this time tomorrow, many of us would be on our way home, if not there already. But there was something else, over and above that, on this warm, clear, still evening. There was a spirit of peace and fulfillment over the stadium. It had been an extraordinary, even historic four days, and while there might be another such conference in the future, there would never be one like this one.

A series of opening prayers came next, and before the final prayer had finished, a sweet, misty sound drifted down from the highest rows in the uppermost tier — it was the sound of singing in the Spirit, and there was a gentleness to it tonight, that made it like an audible rainbow.

The man at the microphone fell silent and lifted his hands, as did the rest of us. We just stood there and worshiped the Lord. And the harmonies of sound that came forth from more than 40,000 hearts expressed to Him what no one could ever hope to put into words.

Jack Brombach, the overall coordinator for the Servants of the Light community in Minneapolis, was the master of ceremonies, and the first speaker he introduced was Catherine Marshall. She told a tragic, moving story of a newly Spirit-baptized couple whose daughter was cruelly abducted and murdered, but who were given in the midst of their grief, a gift of joy from the Holy Spirit, making the point that no matter how rough our circumstances, that supernatural gift is available to each of us.

Following her was Bill Burnett, the Archbishop of Capetown, South Africa. He brought a message of hope: though the Charismatic Renewal was only five or six years old in his country, it was moving with "astonishing rapidity." He pleaded for prayer for his country, for the whites to love and the blacks to forgive, and he praised God that He was going to do the impossible.

There was another song, and then this word of prophecy: "The Lord has a word to speak to the leaders of the Christian churches — to the leaders of *all* the Christian churches — and if you are a bishop, or a superintendent, or a supervisor, or an overseer, or the head of a Christian movement or organization, and that includes many of us here, this word is for you. Because the Lord says, you are all guilty in my eyes for the condition of my people, who are weak and divided and unprepared. I have set you in office over them, and you have not fulfilled that office, as I would have it fulfilled. Because you have not been the servants that I have called you to be. This is a hard word, but I want you to hear it.

"You have not come to me and made important in your lives and in your efforts those things which were most important to me, but instead you chose to put other things first. And you have tolerated division amongst yourselves and grown used to it, and you have not repented for it and fasted for it, or sought me to bring it to an end. But you have tolerated it and increased it. And you have not been my servants first of all in every case, but you have served other people ahead of me, and you have served the world ahead of me, and you have served your organizations ahead of me. But I am God, and you are my servants; why are you not serving me first of all?

"I know your hearts, and I know that many of you love me, and I have compassion on you, and I have placed you in a very high place. But I have placed you there, and I call you to account for it. Now, humble yourselves before me and come to me in repentance, in fasting, mourning and weeping for the condition of my people. Because if you do not humble yourselves now and seek me earnestly, then my people will be unprepared for the difficulties that lie ahead."

There was stunned silence at the completion of this word of prophecy. No applause, and all thought of praising and singing was gone. God had told us how displeased He was at the performance of those He had placed in positions of leadership, but the rest of us, who were not leaders, took every word for ourselves, as well. The moment of repentance had come. He had waited for us to initiate it, and when we wouldn't, He had taken the matter into His own hands. But the word was not finished; the speaker was continuing.

"And I believe the Lord has a further word for us here. I want you to link hands with one another, take hold of the hands of the people next to you. The Lord says to you: stand in unity with one another, and let nothing tear you apart. And by no means separate from one another, through your jealousy and bitterness and your personal preferences, but hold fast to one another. Because I am about to let you undergo a time of severe trial and testing, and you will need to be in unity with one another." And everywhere, people joined hands, stretching across the aisles to do so.

"But I tell you this, also: I am Jesus, the Victor King. And if you hold fast to one another and follow after me, then I will vindicate my holy name on this earth and in the sight of the peoples on this earth. It will be manifest, and it will be clear, and it will be in your lifetimes. Because I am Jesus, the Victor King, and I have promised you victory."

There was a further silence, then much wondrous applause — the assembly's way of saying thank you to God for such a clear and direct word.

And on the heels of this word of prophecy, came another, this time spoken by one of the women in the Word Gifts Group: "I had a vision of this entire stadium kneeling before the Father, and the Lord said to me, humble yourselves this night, my chosen people. Bow before me. Bow before me this night, for I reign among you in power and great majesty. Fall on your knees before me, my people, for I reign among you. Be in awe of my great and terrible majesty. For as you obey me, I will encircle you with a commandment. My people, in days of old, I commanded, and the waters stood apart. This night, my people, I command you: *may these waters come together*. This is my word and my promise, says the Lord."

There was no applause now; every person in the stadium was on his knees.

As we knelt, there came yet another word of prophecy. It

was the last to be heard at the conference, and like the first, it came in verse form. It was so powerful and so moving that one could scarcely breathe as it was being spoken:

Mourn and weep,
   for the body of my Son is broken.
Mourn and weep,
   for the body of my Son is broken.
Come before me with broken hearts and contrite spirits,
   for the body of my Son is broken.
Come before me with sackcloth and ashes,
Come before me with tears and mourning,
   for the body of my Son is broken.

I would have made you one new man,
   but the body of my Son is broken.
I would have made you a light on a mountaintop,
A city glorious and splendorous
     that all the world would have seen,
   but the body of my Son is broken.

The light is dim,
My people are scattered,
   the body of my Son is broken.
I gave all I had
In the body and blood of my Son;
It spilled on the earth,
   the body of my Son is broken.

Turn from the sins of your fathers
And walk in the ways of my Son.
Return to the plan of your Father,
Return to the purpose of your God;
   the body of my Son is broken.
Mourning and weeping,
   for the body of my Son is broken.

The response of the assembly was shock, almost horror, as it might have been, had we beheld the face of the crucified Christ. To have even this glimpse of the Father's grief was more than I could bear. I wept, and so did many others. And I repented for all in me that had done this to Him, and asked His forgiveness for who I was without Him, and determined from that moment to stand with Him, and against self. And I sensed that He heard me and forgave me and intended to help me do just that.

I cannot speak for anyone else, though it seemed that most others were letting the Holy Spirit search their hearts and reveal to them what they needed to see, and what they needed to do about what they had seen. Soon, as the Holy Spirit worked through these things with each one of us, there was a sense of forgiveness and healing taking place, as if a dirty wound were being cleaned out and antiseptic and bandages applied. And I and a great many others also, I suspected, were beginning to feel that absolutely empty, hollowed-out, scoured-out feeling that comes when the Lord has done a deep work of cleansing in us. We had at last gone to the Cross and were in the process of going through it, and into the Resurrection Life with Him.

"The body of my Son is broken — over and over that phrase seemed to echo, and concurrent with the personal repentance, and perhaps made possible by it, another repentance was underway — a corporate repentance. For we, as a body, needed to repent for our part in the brokenness of the larger Body of Christ, for all the divisions in it which we tolerated or abetted, either passively or deliberately. We were asked then, to sing "Father, We Adore You," and I don't think that simple chorus has ever been sung with such feeling.

As we continued to kneel, a message in tongues was delivered by someone in the Word Gifts Group; it may have been the first of the conference. We were asked to sing quietly in the Spirit, until the interpretation came, and when it did, it was not a word-by-word interpretation but rather a picture, which was understood to be a response to Bill Burnett's message. "It was like there was a map of Africa, which grew larger until the focus was on the southern part of Africa. And there'd been some great hurt and great battles fought, and blood that had been shed. And out of this, there rose up a black man and a white man and looked at each other across the carnage and the blood, and they found their way to each other. And they embraced and found one another in the love of Jesus."

There was silence, and then we sang, "Seek Ye First the Kingdom of God." Up on the platform, Bill Burnett knelt with the others, tears streaming down his cheeks, and Vinson Synan came up to comfort him.

Several prayers were prayed next, which gave words to our repentance, and at length Fr. Mike Scanlan was introduced. As he spoke, he leaned forward, balanced on the balls of his feet, like a prize-fighter, and there was a perfect balance of admonition and encouragement in his voice: "My brothers and sisters, do not lose that spirit of repentance. Do not lose that spirit of intercession. For God wants that to continue in your lives. He wants that to be an intimate part of your lives, as you go forth from here. This is not something stopping this moment or in a few moments; this is a way of living that you and I are called to!" And there was a burst of applause.

I believe God wants to tell us something of what He is doing right now, of what He is doing here in this stadium. Because He loves us, He has called us to that repentance and that ongoing intercession. And because He loves us, He has given us the awe-inspiring experience of this week .

Because God loves, He also understands the frustration that we feel this night when faced with the overwhelming task of not only converting our lives to greater fidelity to the Lord, but somehow coming together in a unity of one body that stands forth, and is seen by the world as one!

And therefore they will know that Jesus came, died, rose, poured out His Spirit, and pulled the whole world together in His love, and that that's the kind of power that is His Kingdom in our midst!" And there was thunderous applause.

"The Lord gives us some vision, so that we may be freed of frustration, not to stop repenting or interceding, not to stop praising Him for the awesome mission to which we're called, to bring His body together as one, not to stop working out the solution, but, in fact, so that we *can* do it."

He went on to recall how God had brought unity, when the early Body of Christ was far more perilously split than it was today, and there was no human solution to the separation between Jewish converts and Gentile converts. At that time, God had given Peter — a man who had repented and thus been made ready — a vision that he was to eat what was unclean under Jewish law. And then He took him to the house of Cornelius and showed him that the Gentiles had their Pentecost, just as the Jews did, and that there was only one Pentecost, but it could fall over and over again, in many places. We were to be His Peter, today.

And so we gradually moved through repentance and forgiveness, into that renewed dedication and that clean, spontaneous sunburst of joy that is the gift of the Holy Spirit. There was some good news to be shared, and Vinson Synan shared it: "Last night, the Lord gave us all and more to cover the whole remaining cost of the conference! Last night's offering was $52,100. Now you may ask why should we take another offering tonight . . . There are ten different denominational groups that came together to form this conference, and all of these conferences took a chance of losing support in Kansas City. We have prayed that the Lord would not only give us what we would have had, had we met separately, but that He would give us more than we would have had, had we met separately. And we believe He is going to do this tonight."

He had more good news: he announced the new Charismatic fellowships to great cheering, and then called on us to share the treasures that God had given us. As the usher came down from taking the offering on the speakers' platform, I felt a strong nudge to put all the money I had into his pail — both pockets, *and* the larger bills in my billfold. So I did.

In the meantime, something was happening up on the speakers' platform; Kevin was announcing a change in the program. Rod Lensch, of the Lutheran Charismatic Renewal Service, who was to be the next scheduled speaker, had felt the Holy Spirit leading him to relinquish his time. The planning committee up on the platform had prayed about it and it had witnessed to them that this was of God, and confirmation had come through the Word Gifts Group.

"We want to pray for Rod," Kevin said, "and we accept all the sacrifices and the work and the effort that went into the preparation of his message. We know that God will take that work and use it in ways that we have no idea of, for the building up of His Body and the strengthening of His people. We want to be a people here obedient to the Holy Spirit, and Rod has given us an example tonight from which we must learn, and which we must imitate in our own lives, as we seek to be a more obedient people to the Lord, our God." To which there was great, appreciative applause.

I was really struck by what Rod Lensch had done, and while I knew that God would indeed honor his obedience in a special way, I could sense that it had cost him quite a bit. I wondered if I would have as quickly given up the only opportunity of its kind that I might ever have. But obviously the Holy Spirit was altering the program, as He had in the Messianic Jewish workshop that afternoon.

Just then, Kevin was handed a note, which he looked at a moment, then read aloud. It was a phoned-in message from the President of the United States:

> To all the Christian representatives at the Kansas City Charismatic meeting: I ask your prayers for me, that I may make the right decisions toward bringing about world peace and better understanding between the different nations and those of different beliefs. Please pray for human freedom, and that liberty may be enhanced by the teachings of Christ. Please remember, I need you and your support of prayer in the days to come.

There was applause for the President's message, and the main speaker of the evening was introduced. He was Dr. James Forbes, a black associate professor at Union Theological Seminary in New York. Well-dressed in a conservative but fashionable three-piece suit, Jim Forbes had an appealing sense of humor and a message which got to the heart of the matter. When it came to teaching, homiletics was one of his specialties, "but as hard as I tried to get three points together, I couldn't. The Lord finally gave me three points: *See me*, saith the Lord, was point #1. Point #2: *See me*, saith the Lord. And can you guess what point #3 is? Amen!" And with that, he picked up a theme which had been running through the conference and this evening's prophetic words:

"All through the book of the Revelation of our Lord Jesus Christ, we are constantly called to look above ourselves, constantly called to come up higher, constantly invited to shift our focus from the mundane affairs which perplex us and the threats which stand before us, and the ordeal which shall suddenly come. And we read about the fact that John's warning to the seven churches was that 'something's coming, something's going to happen shortly. But in advance of its coming, I want you to lift your eyes above what shall be, so that when it comes, your vision will have shifted beyond that which perplexes you, so that you will have a chain of reference that will sustain you.' "

And he went on to expand on that chain of reference in terms of the power that was being manifested through the Renewal. "What God hath done in us and is doing in us . . . is exactly what He has created a deep hunger for, in the nation . . . And the Lord is telling us, *see me.* For if we will see God when the hunger of the nation has risen to famine intensity, we will be a people who can help show forth His glory. And that's what we're called to do, to go down from here showing forth that there is a God, there is power right now!"

This note of victory immediately followed by the announcement of a vision received by someone in the Word Gifts Group: "I saw a picture of water pouring from the scoreboard there — it was like water, but it wasn't water — pouring out onto the field and pouring in great volume. It flooded the field and began to lift up the platform here, and as it lifted the platform up and began to fill the stadium, all of you on the sides began to float out into the middle. And as we floated upwards, when we would get to each level, you would float out, and we would become one. We reached the top of the stadium, and it was like a huge punchbowl at a wedding." To which there was a burst of surprised laughter.

"Suddenly, we were all one, and we began to float out the exits. And as we floated out, I could see that what was carrying us was the Holy Spirit. We were not going in our own strength, we were not going in our own ability, but it was the Spirit carrying us out. We were one in the Spirit, and we were floating out." It was reported then, that an identical vision had been received earlier and had been written down and passed to the planning committee though the person who had just shared that vision, had not known of it.

There was only one hymn that could follow such a vision, the same with which the conference had opened: "All Hail the Power of Jesus' Name." And it seemed to me as we sang, that all of the tremendous potential that had lifted that hymn on Wednesday evening, had been realized by Saturday evening. It was hard to believe how much God had accomplished in four days! I knew what He had done in my own life, and as I looked up and around that vast stadium full of joyous Christians for the last time, I knew it was true of thousands upon thousands of others, as well. But no one was consconsciously thinking of all that; we were just putting our hearts into every word. And how beautiful of the Holy Spirit to have given us those great old hymns which could carry the full measure of all that we wanted to express! "Bring forth the royal diadem, and crown Him Lord of all." Jesus, the Victor King!

The joy of that moment was indescribable! The stadium was indeed a wedding punchbowl, brimming over with the joy that would be present at the wedding supper of the Lamb. And it was different from the exuberance of the night before; it was a clean, pure heavenly gift. It was as if the Lord were saying, My children, you have repented and I have forgiven you. You have given me your hearts again and joined them together, one to another. Now drink of my joy, to your hearts' content.

And we did. Nobody was leaving. The main speaker was finished, it was very late, and forty thousand people were staying right where they were, raising their voices as one, in that glorious anthem of praise. Up in the press box, I noticed that nearly all the press corps was on their feet too, and standing near me on the field, the hard-boiled ABC-TV news team was looking around in stunned amazement, their cameras and microphones forgotten. And the scoreboard joined in: "Jesus is Lord, Jesus is Lord," it proclaimed over and over.

From joy, we moved into the final phase of the conference: victory. The song we sang next came from the Renewal in New Zealand, "Lift High the Banners of

Love," and it brought tears of gladness to the eyes of practically everyone. There was a supernatural power and lift to it, and singing it, you *knew* that, in Christ, you could not be beaten, that the Body of Christ was unconquerable and would emerge victorious over whatever was hurled at it. You could almost see the walls of Jericho ahead, shimmering in the noonday heat, as you marched forward to the sound of the trumpets, raising a long column of dust, and keeping pace with the white banners waving along the line.

> The Body of Christ is an army,
> Fighting powers unseen.
> Bringing captives to freedom
> In the name of Jesus, our King.
>
> *Lift high the banners of love, hallelujah,*
> *Sound the trumpets of war;*
> *Christ has gotten us the victory, hallelujah,*
> *Jericho must fall!*

And now, above us the scoreboard was marching the words ALLELUIA, ALLELUIA, ALLELUIA, shoulder to shoulder, as it were, in time to the music and as large as the sign could carry. When the song ended, there was a deafening roar of joy! It was the ultimate moment of victory, the likes of which none of us had ever seen or heard before! But it was a sound we would one day hear again — when the Lord Himself returned in glory!

On and on it went, and then Kevin came forward to pray, his voice breaking with emotion: "Heavenly Father, Father of our Lord Jesus Christ, I'm supposed to pray a closing prayer, O Lord, but with you, there is no ending, only eternal beginning!" And that may have been the first time a prayer was ever interrupted with a great cheer. "O Lord, our God, we praise you, and we bless you, for you have commissioned us to flow forth from this place as a living prophecy . . . and so, Father, in all the confidence of the Spirit, we go forth with your hand upon us to be your body in this world which needs you now, in Jesus' name we pray, (and everyone joined him) *Amen!*"

And then we sang the "Song of Thanks," another with the strong Hebrew flavor which had put so much fire into the music of the conference. In addition to the excitement of the tambourines and the racing of guitars and violins, there was a trilling of flutes above the music and over everything else, a high soprano descant that seemed to be reaching up for the last pinnacle of praise. The cumulative effect was supreme joy, and it was impossible to keep from dancing. If King David was this full of joy, no wonder he danced before the Lord; he couldn't help it!

And so was everyone (except the ushers on the field, who maintained their vigil). Masses of people all around were swaying back and forth together, only this time much faster than before. And up in the long, glass-paneled press box, I noted that they'd linked arms and were dancing there, too. Howard Cosell would be speechless!

The song that followed, the last song of the evening, was even faster — the traditional Jewish "Shalom Aleikhem". We danced with total abandon. A hora line formed along the edge of the field, some fifty yards long, and up on the speakers' platform, they were whirling so, there must have been angels keeping them from going off the sides.

When the song finished another cheer rent the night sky. It was over, but it was glorious — a night no one who was there would ever forget. Inside our hearts, it was still the grand finale of a fourth-of-July fireworks display, but Dick Mishler was obedient to the leading of the Spirit and called for quiet numbers to follow, as we filed out. At the corners of the stadium were huge, descending-spiral ramps down which the people flowed, being carried along by the living water of the unifying Spirit, and gradually coming back down to earth.

I waited at the end of the tunnel to the field, and there came Judson Cornwall. "How about that?" I called to him.

"Oh, glory! If this isn't history, I don't understand history!"

Kevin Ranaghan came next. "How are you going to capture *that* in print?" he called in passing, and I just shook my head.

And then came Fr. Mike Scanlan, and we moved over to the Chiefs' exercise area and stood in the lee of one of the weight machines. Fr. Mike was still a little breathless from the dancing. What did he think of this night? He took a couple of deep breaths and used the time to marshal his thoughts before answering.

"I think it's an extraordinary night, that God has released so much glory, so much presence here! But whenever He does that, you can be sure that He has a deep word of calling for us, and those prophecies tonight were the most demanding prophecies that I've ever heard, back to back. Something's going to happen, and I think what's going to happen is that some of what's been proclaimed is going to fall on rock, and some will be choked by thorns, but a lot of it is going to bear fruit!" He paused and thought a moment.

"There's going to be a new and more powerful ecumenical leadership in unity of Christian life than we have seen in the last five hundred years. And that's going to come from this conference, and it's going to be the most important fruit of the whole conference. I really glory in that; there's just a quiet peace deep within my spirit that it's right, that it's true, and that God has worked through all this. He gives us all the frills and fringes when we rejoice in His glory. And thank God we need His glory, or we couldn't always swallow His words. But He gave us both, and I leave here with more hope for Christianity than at any time in my life."

And that pretty well summed it all up, I thought, as I walked out to the wagon. I turned and took a last look at Arrowhead. People were streaming down the ramps and out the exits, and yet it was still lit up on all levels, vast and imposing in the night, the wedding punchbowl of Jesus, the Victor King.

15

To Serve

We had a passenger, riding back to town with us — an older gentleman who had asked for a lift. He wore glasses and had thinning hair and never entered into our joy — indeed, he never spoke a word. But when we reached the Muehlebach, and everyone piled out, in the rearview mirror I noticed Dean do a very unusual thing. He laid down his notebook and tape recorder on the sidewalk and gave the old gentleman a big bear hug. Dean is about six-three and two-twenty, and has a naturally gruff personality; he just doesn't go around hugging people. So as soon as I got back from parking the car and found him in the line outside the ice cream parlor, I asked him about it.

"I don't know," he frowned, "something just made me do it. And not only that, I told him I loved him." He shook his head. "Right there in the middle of Kansas City! But you know, he started to talk then. He had lived in Belfast, and there's tremendous bitterness there, between the Protestants and the Catholics. He's a Catholic, and he hates Protestants. He knows he shouldn't, but like all of us, he does some things he shouldn't."

We were joined by some more of our gang, and it was a moment before Dean continued. "Well, apparently he had confessed his hatred to God and asked God to forgive him. But he had never asked any Protestant to forgive him, he said, he had never had any contact with one, until me. When I just hugged him, he said it was like a barrier being broken. So he asked me to forgive him, and I said, sure. I went my way, and he went his, but I don't think either of us will be quite the same again," and tears formed in Dean's eyes at the recollection.

We were next at the counter. "Hey, can you buy tonight?" I said to Dean. "I put everything I had into the offering tonight."

Dean laughed. "I was about to ask you the same thing. I gave everything I had to David du Plessis, while you were checking on his departure gate." We both laughed and borrowed the price of a couple of cones from Tom Witter. It was well after one by the time we got to bed, and we had communion the next morning.

I was a little envious of John and Dean going out to Arrowhead, where the Catholics would be celebrating Mass. We had felt that the sight of all those white-robed priests distributing the elements had to be captured on film. But I was an Episcopalian, and it was in the Episcopal service that I belonged. On my way to it, I stopped off to look in at the Messianic Jewish service which was in the lobby of the Little Theatre. The lobby was octagonal and decorated in 1930's modern, which meant that it was mildly mystical — black and white marble tiles, zodiac signs set into the ceiling, white and gilt fixtures — but somehow it had the feeling of an ancient Jewish synagogue and was thus transformed by the Holy Spirit into a singularly appropriate setting.

Certainly there was nothing eerie or mystical about the close little band of some two hundred or so Messianic Jewish worshippers gathered in the center of the octagon. They were there to celebrate the eucharist as their Messiah had called them to, and the music they were singing had the same power to quicken the blood and raise the spirits as I had noticed throughout the conference. With a jolt, I was reminded that this was not the Mass I was supposed to be attending.

I guess I was a little apprehensive about the Episcopal service, that my own denomination wouldn't measure up. I needn't have been; it was beautiful! On the stage of the Music Hall were at least forty priests all in white cassocks with red stoles, and behind them was, in my admittedly biased opinion, the best-looking banner of the conference. Against a backdrop of dark velvet theatre curtains, this enormous red-orange banner with the white dove descending made a striking effect in the darkened theatre. And the music provided by the Alleluia Company was as good as any we had heard.

The first of two unforgettable moments in that service came when Bob Hawn, the principal celebrant, announced his offering. It was one of the briefest appeals of its kind I had ever heard: "Give as you would to Jesus, if you could stand His searching look; give as you would to Jesus, if His hand, your offering took." I was glad that I had cashed a check that morning, so I could empty my wallet again.

The other moment came during the preparation of the elements. The music group sang a simple, quiet Spanish song, *Jesus Mi Rey*, with a slow, deliberate pace. It was a haunting melody that drifted into the corners of the theatre and seemed to linger there. And the Holy Spirit used this music to evoke a sweetness and gentleness of spirit that wasn't sorrow — just a yearning to be as close to Jesus as possible, and to somehow blend with Him. At the height of it, Bob elevated the host. His eyes were closed, his face radiant — almost beatific, if such a word can be used. He was communing with Christ, and by his proxy, so were we. In speechless reverence, we were transported out of the theatre and into His eternal presence.

Later, waiting in line for communion, I thanked God for having been there. There was prophecy, prayer for Bishops Burnett and Chiu, and then the service — and the conference — was over.

That afternoon, while Dean de-briefed a couple of people who were helping us, I checked out the banquet that the CRS was providing for all the workers. It was set up in the ballroom in which the Presbyterians had been having Holy Communion, just a few hours before. Now, it was all gleaming white tablecloths accented with red napkins, and a raised head table, at which would sit all the division leaders and their wives. It was going to be a festive affair, and I asked Phil Haney about it. "We try to give them a really nice meal, where they can relax, and just say a few thank-yous to them, and then they can be on their way. Let somebody else serve them, for a change.... They worked hard, long hours, day and night, and they were always joyful and took their assignment and did it. And that's what counts."

The workers began coming in now, and as they filled the tables, I saw Kay Frey and asked her if the conference had fulfilled her expectations. "Oh gosh, it was way beyond them! It was a blessing, I think, for all of us who worked on it. But you know, Paul De Celles, the overall coordinator of our community, told us before we came, that the People of Praise were going to Kansas City, not to be blessed by the conference, but to serve at the conference. And that was really the best attitude to come with, because we were very, very busy, but very peaceful, because we were here for a purpose: to serve."

I thanked Kay and saw Joe Stante then, and wondered how it had gone with all those children. "We had 850, like we'd expected, and it was absolutely wonderful! The Lord just really took care of us . . . . Like one noontime, the company that was supplying the meals forgot to put any drinks in the meals. We notified them, and as quickly as they could, they sent up eight gallons of some kind of fruit punch. Fortunately, some two hundred of the kids were at the zoo, but eight gallons could not begin to take care of all those who were left. But they started filling glasses and passing them out, and somehow there was a glass for every kid that was there, and all the workers and adult staff, too. It was a miracle!"

When all the tables were filled, Kevin Ranaghan summed up the meaning of the conference for them and the part they had played. "It's the planning committee, the denominational boards, and the speakers who receive a very public recognition. But *all* our gifts, whether speaking or ushering or whatever kind of service we're performing, come from the Holy Spirit . . . . I know that the Lord is well pleased at your obedience and your service, and the administration of this conference is extremely grateful for the very, very hard work we know that all of you have done."

Dean returned then, and he had a miracle of his own to report. One of the people whom we had asked to help us gather material was a friend of mine from my first visit to Kansas City, Harry Lunn, who had done some free-lance work for *Logos*. When Dean and I had briefed Harry before the conference, his eyes had been giving him a problem; he kept blinking and squinting, and it was difficult for him to gaze steadily at anything.

Thursday morning, Harry had been at the Nondenominational A conference. At the conclusion of the meeting, Harry had gone forward to greet one of the speakers, when standing next to him, he saw a man with whom he had been out of fellowship for several years. "Out of fellowship" was putting it mildly; Harry was embittered. He started to turn and walk away, but the Holy

Spirit said, No, go and speak to him. Harry pushed the thought aside, but it came back, much stronger than before. It was no longer a nudge; it was a command.

He went over and spoke to the man casually, and abruptly the man wrapped his arms around Harry and hugged him. Stunned, Harry hugged him back, and in that instant, "there was a flash of light that absolutely blinded me. I couldn't see a thing! And next I felt this white-hot, unendurable heat — but no pain. And then it was over, and I wondered, 'What on earth was that?' And I felt a surge of inexpressible love for this man and the others he was associated with. He asked me to forgive him for his part in what had happened, and I did and asked him to tell all the others that I loved them in Christ. And I really did! I've never felt such love!"

"Well, you certainly look like a different person, Harry!" Dean exclaimed. "Do you notice it?"

"Oh, praise God!" was all Harry could say.

Recounting the incident to me, Dean said that Harry's eyes were clear and bright and steady, and his whole face and manner seemed more at peace. (Harry visited me on Cape Cod just recently, and I saw for myself. The softness and the peace had continued to deepen in the intervening weeks. There were still traces of the old Harry, to be sure, but there was no mistaking that this was a whole new man in Christ. It was as big a miracle of healing as any of the many physical healings that had taken place in Kansas City, and it had happened because two men had been willing to put the past behind them and be made one by the Holy Spirit.)

That Sunday afternoon, the temperature in Kansas City soared to a hundred and two degrees, but nearly everyone had gone home before the heat reached its peak. Indeed, after the press of people which had thronged the streets around the Municipal Auditorium, to see no one at all on foot, and hardly any cars in the streets, was almost eerie. It was like a ghost town; there was even a sheet from a discarded newspaper, blowing across Wyandotte.

The next morning, we went over to the conference office for the last time, to drop off and pick up some things, and it, too, seemed strangely deserted, though of course, the last time we had been there was D-Day plus two, when the action was at its peak. There were still a few people around, and Jim Harcus was one of them. Astonished, I realized that I had almost forgotten about the book! "How'd we do, Jim?" I almost didn't want to ask.

We haven't got Sunday's counted yet, but you're close to six thousand. I wouldn't be at all surprised if you reach seven, when they're all done coming in."

I just shook my head, unable to speak. The Lord had told us in the beginning that it would be five to six thousand at the conference. He was faithful. I turned away, so Jim wouldn't see me. And then I smiled. God had not said anything about orders coming in *after* the conference, because we didn't need to know that. All we needed to know was that there would be enough to start. (As I write this, we have received around 7500 orders!)

We next talked to Dan De Celles. Now that it was over, what had been their biggest crises — the ones we *hadn't* heard about? He told us about the scoreboard, which had been out of commission as late as Wednesday morning, and the bus-loading area which had to be changed at the last minute, and their phone system going on the fritz just before the conference began. And he laughed. "By this time, it was clear where it was coming from. Of course, we made mistakes and forgot things, but these things were of an order and magnitude that were just not human error. It was coming from the Devil. And as he always does, he overplayed his hand. We started praying accordingly, and we had no more real disasters after that. God was in charge. The people in the stands had no idea that anything was wrong, and that was even more of a miracle to me personally — the peace and order that people experienced at this conference, when you considered the magnitude of the problems before hand. We had done all we could, working as hard as we could, and it wasn't enough. It was God who would have to turn it around, and He did."

That peace and order, I thought to myself as we thanked him, was also in part a reflection on the preparation, both the staff's and the planning committee's. Thinking of the planning committee made me think of all the extremely positive reactions we had gotten from those who had served on it. As Ross Whetstone later told me: "I remember sitting there one day, just sort of observing the group and reflecting on my position in it, and my gratitude for being there, and thinking that while this group of people was very much like our executive types in the Methodist church that I'd sat with for years, at the same time, it was radically different, because of the warmth of the brotherhood that we felt there, and the feeling that we were involved in something that God was doing right now, and needed to wait upon God for direction almost moment by moment, as we proceeded with our work . . . .

"It was something quite unique. I was a pastor for twenty-eight years and a denominational executive for nine years and am now on the college scene, so I have a long background against which to put this and develop a perspective on it, and that warmth and affection was different, not in kind but in degree; it was more intense than in any group I've ever been in."

If unity in the Body of Christ was going to happen, it would have to begin with the leadership, and as a cross-section of that leadership, the planning committee had demonstrated that not only was it possible, but it bore fruit of inestimable value.

Larry Christenson later shared the reaction of one of the young women in his congregation who had attended: "She said, 'You know, I've always felt a little inhibited in worship, a little stiff,' and she said, 'there was such a freedom in worship. The reason we were able to do that was because we had such confidence in our leaders.' She was referring to the planning committee, sitting up on the stage. 'They set the pace, and we were able to follow.' "

Unity was up to each of us, of course, but the leaders had a special responsibility . . . .

Fr. Ed Sylvia, who had been the facility manager for Arrowhead, came into the office at that moment, and we asked him if he had experienced any situations in which he had been clearly given a helping hand by the Almighty. "Well, we never did have enough ushers to fill all the positions, but it was funny — even before the conference, I had a sense that the Lord was gathering angels here in Kansas City ahead of time and was setting up camp all around Arrowhead. And in that particular area of personnel, I think the Lord just covered us and really had angels where we couldn't have people."

How about the professional manager of the stadium — how did he feel about the conference? "Bob Wachter? Why don't you call him and ask him?"

So we did. He was a cheerful fellow, and the first thing he noted was that it was a very clean crowd. "I mean, they picked up their trash. And the conference staff has a bunch of people out here now, cleaning up anything that might be left behind. Yup, they kept the stadium very clean; we'd like to have them back."

And we got a similar response from the mayor, when we called him. "We're delighted with the conference's success," he said, "and we haven't heard anything but praises for their enthusiasm."

Just before we said our last round of goodbyes, we were told of the pastor of a local Catholic church, whom the conference — and the Charismatic Renewal — had taken somewhat by surprise. He had not had any close contact with Charismatics, and their sincerity and caring had both touched and puzzled him.

Dean said, "You know, why don't we interview him, on our way out of town?"

"I was just thinking the same thing," I said. "Let's go."

And so we took a last look around the old sub, said our goodbyes, and took the slowest elevator down for the last time.

16

Homeward

Fr. Demming was in, when we stopped by his office, and he did have some time he could give us. He was middle-aged, gracious, and judging from the titles of the books that lined his shelves, intellectually inclined.

We asked him about the conference and what he thought of it, and he was very frank. He said that in the months before it actually began, he had some strong reservations about it, because it seemed like it was being handled extremely haphazardly, with no advance team in town, working out the details weeks beforehand. In fact, when he heard that the bulk of the CRS team was arriving only a week beforehand, he went to the bishop of the diocese and said, "Bishop, they're going to be an embarrassment to the Church and to the diocese and the city — it just can't work. I believe in the Holy Spirit, but I think you've got to do your homework!"

But for some reason, the bishop had not been overly concerned, and so Fr. Demming had resigned himself to the situation. Church business took him out of town until the day after the conference had begun. "I had received the program, of course, but I really didn't pay too much attention to it. At our noon mass, we usually have sixty to sixty-five people, but with the conference in town, and this being the first full day and all, I thought we might have perhaps 150 to 200 people."

Fr. Demming leaned back in his chair. "I'd gone out that morning and was a little late getting back, so I went right into the sacristy — and there were twenty priests there! Well, I was very happy to have them; I think we're always happy to have other priests to help, but nothing prepared me for the shock of going out to Mass and seeing twelve or thirteen hundred people there! It was just great, but it really kind of stripped me of everything else. I hadn't prepared anything to say to them, so I just really welcomed them.

"And the Mass went off fine, as if we'd planned it for weeks. That afternoon, at the five-fifteen Mass, we had a large crowd also, and so I told them about a funeral service we were having the next day for a ninety-one-year-old lady who had died and really had no relatives. There were just two nieces, neither of whom was able to come, and so I invited them to come to that, if they liked."

He shook his head at the recollection. "We're a downtown church here, and mostly the people who come are older folks, retired people. Normally there might be five or so people who would come to a funeral like that, but do you know that that day there were a thousand people there to pray for that lady?"

We said nothing, but without looking, I knew Dean was as touched as I was.

"Saturday morning was a repeat of Friday," Fr. Demming went on, "and on Saturday morning there was an article in the paper that really expressed what the feeling of Kansas City was, in reference to all those who were there. I think they used the term that they were genuinely nice people, and that's a lot for the *Star* to say. You know, I've never really read an article in there like that." And I recalled the lead headline on the front page: *City Enjoying Biggest, Cleanest, Happiest Rally.*

"I know I was deeply moved," Fr. Demming said. "I think it's probably deeply affected my life and has caused a lot of introspection on my part, humility maybe . . . I went to Arrowhead Saturday night . . . I've never met or seen a more joyous or sincere, kind, good, pure people . . . . It's almost like you've come into contact with something that's kind of unbelievable . . . . In fact, I left Arrowhead just as it was ending." He paused, and I thought of that victorious moment.

"I stood and looked down." Fr. Demming resumed, as if he were seeing it again. "I couldn't see the field from where I stood, but I could see the people. They were standing and singing and dancing, all of that, and to the people I was with, I said, 'You know, I don't really feel like that. But I wish I did.' I looked at the people's faces at Arrowhead, and I was extremely impressed. It was just like people should act at the *parousia*, the second coming of our Lord. If He came here upon earth today, that's how it should be."

We talked some more, and we suggested a couple of books that he might read and thanked him very much for his time. Neither of us felt any leading to say more than that at that time, but on the way out to the car, I suggested to Dean that we stop into the chapel for a moment and pray for Fr. Demming. So we did. On the way out, I noticed that you could make a small contribution and light a candle for someone. I'd never done anything like that before, but it seemed right, and so I did.

A few minutes later, we were on I-70, heading west under a heavy gray sky. The sky matched my spirit, I thought, as we rode along. Dean was driving, but I was too tired to sleep, and I was down, no doubt because I had been high all week long. Already Kansas City was out of sight behind us, and there was a temptation to think of it as a dream — a magnificent but totally unreal dream. Would we really be able to take the heart of those incredible four days home and start living it? Would that new sense of oneness carry with us?

As if in answer, a horn honked to the left of us, and alongside us in the passing lane was another eastbound wagon, filled with a happy family. They waved and pointed skywards, and then held up that familiar bright-orange program. I laughed and held ours up, too.

And that was a scene that repeated itself more than once on the way home.